African Linguistics after #RhodesMustFall

Hannah Gibson • Jacqueline Lück
Kristina Riedel • Savithry Namboodiripad

African Linguistics after #RhodesMustFall

Contextualising the Role of African Languages
in Higher Education in Times of Global Change

Hannah Gibson
Department of Language and Linguistics
University of Essex
Colchester, Essex, UK

Kristina Riedel
Department of Linguistics
University of the Witwatersrand
Johannesburg, South Africa

Jacqueline Lück
Department of Linguistics and Applied Linguistics
Nelson Mandela University
Gqeberha, South Africa

Savithry Namboodiripad
Department of Linguistics
University of Michigan–Ann Arbor
Ann Arbor, MI, USA

This publication was jointly supported by the University of Essex's Open Access Fund and funding from the University of Michigan.

ISBN 978-3-031-74816-5   ISBN 978-3-031-74817-2   (eBook)
https://doi.org/10.1007/978-3-031-74817-2

© The Editor(s) (if applicable) and The Author(s), under exclusive licence to Springer Nature Switzerland AG 2025. This book is an open access publication.

Open Access This book is licensed under the terms of the Creative Commons Attribution 4.0 International License (http://creativecommons.org/licenses/by/4.0/), which permits use, sharing, adaptation, distribution and reproduction in any medium or format, as long as you give appropriate credit to the original author(s) and the source, provide a link to the Creative Commons license and indicate if changes were made.

The images or other third party material in this book are included in the book's Creative Commons license, unless indicated otherwise in a credit line to the material. If material is not included in the book's Creative Commons license and your intended use is not permitted by statutory regulation or exceeds the permitted use, you will need to obtain permission directly from the copyright holder.

The use of general descriptive names, registered names, trademarks, service marks, etc. in this publication does not imply, even in the absence of a specific statement, that such names are exempt from the relevant protective laws and regulations and therefore free for general use.

The publisher, the authors and the editors are safe to assume that the advice and information in this book are believed to be true and accurate at the date of publication. Neither the publisher nor the authors or the editors give a warranty, expressed or implied, with respect to the material contained herein or for any errors or omissions that may have been made. The publisher remains neutral with regard to jurisdictional claims in published maps and institutional affiliations.

Cover pattern © Melisa Hasan

This Palgrave Macmillan imprint is published by the registered company Springer Nature Switzerland AG.
The registered company address is: Gewerbestrasse 11, 6330 Cham, Switzerland

If disposing of this product, please recycle the paper.

Acknowledgements

We are grateful to the respondents who completed the survey as well as those who helped us to circulate the survey around their wider networks. The authors would also like to thank everyone who gave us feedback on drafts of the survey prior to circulation and earlier drafts of this manuscript, including Laura Bailey, Anthony Struthers-Young, Kelly Wright, Hope Morgan, Colin Reilly, Chanel van der Merwe. We would like to thank the anonymous reviewer who provided comments on the entire draft manuscript. Thanks also go to Calle Börstell for providing code which helped to create Fig. 2.1.

We would also like to thank our students, colleagues and friends with whom we discussed many of the issues that emerge in the book. You have all been instrumental in shaping our views on these topics, as well as inspiring us to keep the discussion—and most importantly the work—moving forward.

Contents

1 Introduction: African Linguistics After #RhodesMustFall 1

2 The Survey, the Respondents and Us 23

3 Student and Staff Experiences of African Languages in Higher Education 43

4 Prominence and Erasure of African Languages in Higher Education 61

5 The Role of African Languages in Transformation and Decolonisation 75

6 Views on Decoloniality and Transformation Discourses in African Linguistics 91

7 Conclusions, Next Steps and a Call to Action 109

Appendix 119

References 123

Index 131

About the Authors

Hannah Gibson is Professor of Linguistics at the University of Essex, UK. Her work is primarily concerned with linguistic variation with a focus on African languages, language contact, multilingualism and the link between linguistics and social justice.

Jacqueline Lück is Senior Lecturer in the Department of Linguistics and Applied Linguistics and Deputy Dean in the Faculty of Humanities at Nelson Mandela University, South Africa. Her research interests are language, knowledge and academic literacies; identity, discourse and ideology; decolonisation of linguistics and the curriculum.

Kristina Riedel is Senior Lecturer in the Department of Linguistics at the University of the Witwatersrand, South Africa. Her research is focused on the syntax of the Bantu languages, and also the decolonisation and transformation of Linguistics in South Africa.

Savithry Namboodiripad is Assistant Professor in Linguistics at the University of Michigan-Ann Arbor, USA. Her research concerns contact-induced change and syntactic typology, and how language ideologies and use in multilingual and recently colonised contexts contribute to language change.

List of Figures

Fig. 2.1 A visualisation of where survey respondents were based; size of circle represents frequency — 26

Fig. 2.2 Stacked bar plot of participants' role in academia based on whether or not they are located in Africa — 29

Fig. 5.1 Stacked bar plots representing the valence of participants' responses to: "What role do you think studying and learning about African languages plays in processes of decolonisation, teaching for social justice or transformation?" — 84

Fig. 5.2 Stacked bar plot of valence of response by whether or not participants currently live in Africa — 85

Fig. 5.3 Stacked bar plot of valence of response by current location, broken down into broad global regions — 86

Fig. 5.4 Stacked bar plot of valence of response by whether participants grew up speaking an African Language — 87

LIST OF TABLES

Table 2.1	Participants' current location, coded for uniformity based on open-ended responses	27
Table 2.2	Participants' role in academia	29
Table 2.3	Participants' self-reported gender, aggregated based on open-ended responses	30
Table 2.4	Participants' self-reported race/ethnicity, aggregated based on open-ended responses	31
Table 5.1	Valence of participants' responses to: "What role do you think studying and learning about African languages plays in processes of decolonisation, teaching for social justice or transformation of higher education?"	82

CHAPTER 1

Introduction: African Linguistics After #RhodesMustFall

Abstract This chapter provides a background to the study and the broader context in which the survey was conducted. It introduces the motivation behind the work, which was to examine views related to African languages and decolonisation and transformation. It provides a short overview of the #RhodesMustFall movement in South Africa and highlights parallels with a number of related social justice movements such as #RhodesMustFallOxford and Black Lives Matter. The chapter ends with an overview of the book as a whole, foregrounding a number of the key themes that emerge.

Keywords #RhodesMustFall • Decolonisation • Transformation • African languages • Linguistics

1.1 Background to the Study

This book has its origins in a survey we conducted in 2021. The four of us had been discussing the link between African languages/linguistics and processes of decolonisation and transformation for some time. However, a call for papers for a conference and the initial idea to present a talk on the topic of 'African linguistics after #RhodesMustFall' gathered momentum and saw us come together as scholars and activists to conduct the study on which the current research is based. We were interested in the link between a range of social justice movements that had been taking place globally in recent years, and the role and place of African languages and linguistics in higher education.

It would be easy to write a sentence such 'as 2020 was a year that saw tremendous upheaval'. We could be talking about the Covid-19 pandemic or the 'racial reckoning' that took place across much of North America and parts of Europe. We could be talking about issues and events that shaped our own lives and our own thinking. In many ways we talk to and from all of these places and events. However, we also speak as individuals who have been involved in work on decolonisation and transformation before this and whose work has brought us face-to-face with issues of inequality, awareness of racism, and the erasure and absence of African languages in education in the various contexts in which we live and work.

We developed an online survey that was designed to explore views relating to the link between African languages and linguistics on the one hand, and processes of decolonisation and transformation on the other hand. We were interested in whether our insights into the potential role and place of African languages and linguistics in processes of broader social change were shared by other educators and students in different contexts.

The four of us are involved in teaching topics related to language and linguistics. Conversations with each other and in different contexts had made us increasingly aware of the under-representation of African languages in high education curriculum and in higher educational contexts more broadly. This perception is particularly noteworthy given that two of the authorial team are based at institutions in Africa. This realisation is also linked to wider patterns and observations related to decolonisation and transformation which continue to shape higher education globally. We had views and opinions; we had our own impressions and anecdotes. However, we wanted to know whether these views were shared more widely. We also wanted to know how this issue was experienced differently in a range of places and by diverse groups and communities. We further wanted to see what experiences and ideas our survey respondents had to share about the potential for African languages and linguistics to be part of a broader transformation and decolonial move. Could it in some way also be part of a broader consciousness or awareness raising process?

The survey sought to explore to what extent African languages are present in higher educational institutions both inside and outside Africa, to what extent African languages are part of the curriculum at universities, as well as what exposure students have to African languages beyond linguistics, for example in their history classes or literature classes. We were also interested in what educators and students perceive as the role or link between African languages and processes such as transformation and decolonisation. The potential of language and language study to contribute towards decolonisation has often been described from a historical perspective, so we were interested in people's views on its role in present and ongoing movements of change that seek to improve equality of access, address imbalances and see the development of new governance structures.

A note is in order here on terminology. Understandings and interpretations of decolonisation and transformation are varied and diverse, and have been the subject of extensive debate and theorisation. Indeed, the question of how linguists understand these terms was one of the research questions which motivated our survey, and the results of this question are discussed in Chap. 6. We do not seek to add to the theoretical debate here and as such, we adopt an approach which is influenced by the idea—articulated by Bhambra et al. (2018)—that decolonisation efforts are united by two key political and methodological considerations. Firstly, decolonisation proceeds from a shared way of thinking about the world which takes colonialism, empire, and racism as its empirical and discursive objects of study; and seeks to resituate these phenomena as key shaping forces in the contemporary world where their role has systematically and perpetually been hidden and erased from majority discourses. Secondly, in so doing, decolonisation purports to offer alternative ways of thinking about the world and an alternative form of praxis (Bhambra et al. 2018). A decolonial approach requires us to first recognise how dominant and "unmarked" ways of understanding and interacting with the world have been shaped by these historical forces, and secondly means that we must reimagine and reinvent these practices, while also addressing material and epistemological harms (Gibson et al. 2024).

The focus of the current study extends beyond South Africa. However, we were also inspired by a previous piece of work which surveyed South African linguistics and language instructors and departments (de Vos and Riedel 2023). Their survey showed that instructors reported being involved in curriculum transformation but that in their views these efforts often remain partial. For example, instructors added examples from Bantu languages to otherwise English-centric teaching materials but did not consider including "Khoisan"[1] languages in their curricula. Such efforts

---

[1] While the vast majority of South Africans speak one or more Bantu languages as their first languages, 'Khoisan' languages were spoken across much of the region before colonisation

seemed partial and, in some cases, tokenistic. However, these observations also gave rise to further questions related to how best to empower and support instructors to make meaningful reform in their curricula and to carry out broader fundamental changes that would truly reflect a move towards a decolonised or transformed curriculum and teaching context.

Readers who are less familiar with the South African context might not be used to the term 'transformation' as we used it here and as it is used in relation to South African higher education. In South Africa, transformation has been the prevalent term used since the end of apartheid and the transition to democracy. 'Transformation' in this sense relates to broad institutional and social change to achieve social, economic and educational equity and redress for the injustices of the apartheid and colonial eras. We used the term transformation in this sense in the survey and were in turn also interested in better understanding our participants' responses and views of the term. In this book therefore, we consider transformation to be a broader concept than decolonisation, but also consider it to be an associated movement.

Discussions related to decolonisation have been happening in many disciplinary spaces, including within fields of linguistics. In this way, this work is a small piece of larger movements. However, as discussed in the subsequent sections of this introduction, the global, often student-led, activism in the past five years has spurred a new set of actions within disciplinary spaces where theorising about decoloniality has not traditionally been the norm. As a result, different sub-disciplines of linguistics have also engaged with these issues in different ways. For example, Gibson et al. (2024), examine the colonial underpinnings in the specific case study of syntax—an area of linguistics concerned with the internal organisation of language. The study of syntax includes, for example, the ways in which words can be ordered in phrases and sentences, and the broader structure of a language. Gibson et al. (2024) claim that while syntax has been positioned as a central component of modern linguistics, the history of syntax is intrinsically connected with broader positivist movements in linguistics which have valued moves away from studying language in context and

---

and several 'Khoisan' languages are still spoken in Southern Africa today (Eberhard et al. 2023). A transformed curriculum should in our view not only make reference to majority languages. We use the term 'Khoisan' here, as in de Vos and Riedel's survey, despite the fact that the languages it refers to do not form a genetic group (cf. Güldemann 2014) and that the term itself remains contested. See Witzlack-Makarevich and Nakagawa (2019) for a discussion of the terms used.

towards scientism. One of the consequences of this is that syntax seems to lag yet further behind other sub-disciplines in linguistics in terms of addressing issues of race and racism and the way in which it has contributed to—and continues to uphold—racist assumptions about knowledge and power on a global level. These are notions to which we return in the current book with a view to better understanding the link between language and colonisation, and language and decolonisation which lies at the heart of our work here.

In this way, it is our hope that this short book forms part of ongoing discussions in linguistics and related disciplines about the role and place played by our field in shaping and contributing to decolonial and transformation discourses. Our goal is to both contribute to the discussions through sharing insights and findings from the present study, as well as to spark further discussion and additional research into the area.

1.2 The #RhodesMustFall Movement

The year 2015 saw student-led protests under the title #RhodesMustFall spread across universities in South Africa. The movement started as a protest against a statue of Cecil Rhodes on the University of Cape Town (UCT) campus. This developed into a wider movement calling for the 'decolonisation' of education across South Africa and ultimately gained global momentum. In the same way that Cecil Rhodes was seen by many as a symbol of British imperialism in South Africa, students and staff at universities in other contexts also began questioning names and statues that are found in their institutions more widely. Later, in 2015 and 2016, the closely linked #FeesMustFall movement spread from the University of the Witwatersrand to UCT and Rhodes University and to other institutions across South Africa. While the initial focus was on a proposed increase to tuition fees, the movement also saw this as intimately connected to a reduction in government support for higher education, the slow pace of transformation in South Africa, and broader issues of inequality.

#RhodesMustFall and associated movements triggered discussions of decolonising higher education in South Africa. In the South African context, the focus had been on transformation, a concept related to decolonisation but one that is potentially broader, though both terms are frequently used interchangeably in the South African discourse.[2] Universities South Africa (2015: 2) defines transformation as "a comprehensive, deep-rooted and ongoing social process seeking to achieve a fundamental reconstitution and development of our universities to reflect and promote the vision of a democratic society". Transformation of higher education in South Africa was initially primarily framed by government institutions as achieving equity and parity of access. These policies had a significant impact on creating and widening access for Black students and staff to historically White universities (which we turn to below). Later policy documents addressed success as well as access. It was not enough to open the doors of learning without looking at student success rates and throughput, with some more scrutiny on curriculum issues such as the marginalisation and neglect of African languages (Department of Higher Education and Training 2013). Curriculum offerings required more responsiveness to national priorities and to address concerns of local and regional relevance.

The nation-wide student movements and global events created some urgency for South African institutions of higher learning and academics to reassess their modes of teaching, learning and research. Decolonisation discourses became more commonplace. Discourses of decolonisation in education are not new, neither are student movements, which were a key part of the resistance against apartheid (Reddy 2004) and continued from the 1990s to the present (Cele and Koen 2003) as South Africa grappled with a very slowly changing society, especially at previously disadvantaged institutions which see student protests very regularly. Questioning of a Eurocentric curriculum may in fact be traced back all the way to 1897, when William Wellington Gqoba, an early isiXhosa writer in South Africa, wrote of being taught European history despite never having seen or experienced it (Maseko 2018).

While the general focus on decolonising the curriculum in South African higher education started after #RhodesMustFall, these conversations took place in other parts of Africa and elsewhere as early as the 1950s and 1960s. For example, Falola (2020) describes how members of the Ibadan School of History engaged with Eurocentric racism in the 1950s and Makerere University called for review of the relevance of their

---

[2] We also asked participants to reflect on the link (and the differences) between decolonisation and transformation in our survey. There have also been wider discourses of resistance and push-back against notions of decolonisation in particular.

curriculum after student demonstrations in 1966 (Mamdani 2019). In the United States, W.E.B. Du Bois' Atlanta School of Sociology was an example of liberatory education that challenged core intellectual constructs of racism in science (Morris 2020). Furthermore, the seminal text *Decolonising the Mind* by Ngũgĩ wa Thiong'o referenced the treasures of African language as absent in a classroom marked by "psychological violence" (Ngũgĩ wa Thiong'o 1986: 9).

From the post-apartheid period to the early 2000s, a number of policies were enacted which were meant to bring about transformation in higher education in South Africa. The first significant act of the 2001 National Plan on Higher Education (Department of Education 2001) was to restructure racialised and fragmented institutions to create a single national system that would be non-racial in nature and give access to all (Reddy 2004). This led to a series of mergers between formerly White institutions and Historically Black Institutions (HBIs) and former technical colleges creating a number of multi-campus institutions across the country, including the University of Johannesburg, the University of Kwa-Zulu Natal and the University of the Free State.

There was also a significant change in student demographics. As of 2019, across South African higher education as a whole, 77% of enrolled students identified as Black, which fairly closely matches the 81% South African population which identifies as Black (Council on Higher Education 2021: 15). However, while Black students now constitute the numerical majority in higher education in South Africa, the enrolment rate of Black students has remained lower compared to other racial groups. In 2021, the Black student participation rate was 5.3% while that of White students was 24.6% of the total population group aged 18 to 29 (Statista 2023). Moreover, completion and success rates, and participation in postgraduate education have not shifted significantly. Transformation of academic staff demographics has also lagged behind. For example, Breetzke and Hedding (2018) show that between 2005 and 2015 the percentage of Black faculty at any level in South Africa had only increased by 10% to about 35%. At the same time White faculty still made up about 50% of the faculty overall and about 70% at the rank of professor (Breetzke and Hedding 2018: 154).

As also noted above, student protests have been a regular feature of South African public higher education for decades, going back to the apartheid era and continuing into the democratic era (Badat 2016a, b). Extended protests or those which involved damage to infrastructure have frequently led to particular campuses or universities closing down for periods of time. The protests and the shutdowns take a heavy toll on students and staff when for example the semester dates are adjusted as a result and teaching and learning and research activities, and of course the lives of students and staff are disrupted. Students, staff or other community members have been injured either due the protest actions or from policing (which has included shooting at student protestors with rubber bullets), and in rare cases there have been fatalities. Private security interventions and policing of student protests are at times heavy-handed and thus exacerbate the situation. Students suspected of causing damage to infrastructure or at times for violating injunctions that universities obtain seeking to limit protest actions might be arrested. Universities also lose infrastructure, for example when lecture venues are set on fire (Govender 2016). The protests also take a mental and emotional toll on students and staff, whether they are active participants or not.

Since South Africa became a democracy, student protests have happened most regularly at HBIs (Davids and Waghid 2016; Badat 2016a, b), many of which remain under-resourced and which cater for the most disadvantaged and marginalised students. These protests often affect a single institution or one campus of a multi-campus university. However, the scale of the protests in 2015 and 2016 meant that numerous campuses across South Africa were affected, with several shutdowns for weeks at a time. In contrast to a number of previous shutdowns, it was also the most prestigious, formerly White institutions which were amongst the most affected.

Students' visceral response to their curricula as expressed in the 2015 and 2016 student movements triggered campus conversations about the need for policies to bring about curricular transformation. The response by the South African government, higher education institutions, academics and scholarly societies (cf. de Vos and Riedel 2023 on the responses of the linguistics associations of South Africa) was swift and in some ways also pervasive. Changes were made to student funding, a number of public institutions which had been dual-medium in English and Afrikaans dropped Afrikaans as a medium of instruction, and all universities added decolonisation and curriculum reform to their policies in some form. However, as normal academic life returned, the resultant changes were often limited to policies, plans, and committees that did not radically change South African higher education. As Sara Ahmed describes in the context of policies aimed at promoting diversity at UK institutions:

> If we consider the politics of documenting diversity, we can see that documents create fantasy images of the organizations they apparently describe. The document says 'we are diverse', as if saying it makes it so. In a way, our task must be to refuse to read such documents as doing what they say. That is not to say that such documents do not matter, or that they do not do important work. They do. (Ahmed 2007: 607)

The creation of such "fantasy images" can also be seen to apply to transformation and decolonisation plans and policies, as well as similar documents and committees in South Africa and elsewhere. Jansen and Walters (2022) analyse what has changed since the #RhodesMustFall protests and argue that only some of the South African public institutions which saw widespread student protests tried to comprehensively address the calls to decolonise the curriculum, often with limited impact.

The impact of the Covid-19 pandemic may also have exacerbated already high levels of inequality and derailed attempts to decolonise the curriculum in South Africa. With the emergency online shifts globally during the Covid-19 outbreak, already extant digital divides were cast into sharp relief and these were compounded by a largely monolingual English online learning space. The decolonisation project appears to have stalled as a result of Covid-19, as students and instructors needed to learn how to teach and be online. In addition, many South African students struggled to engage with learning and teaching provisions due to a lack of access to technology and mobile phone data which would enable access to online learning spaces. We are, however, cautiously hopeful that some of these processes and tools can contribute to positive changes in higher education, provided that academics do what Ahmed (2007) describes as refusing to treat policies as completions of the work but demand their implementation and evaluation.

Humanities and Social Science disciplines are often considered to be more temporal and porous to decolonisation while 'universal truths' in the natural sciences and its traditional modes of doing have at times been presented as not in need of change or update. Zembylas (2018) argues for a differentiated approach to decolonisation as inclusive of (i) a soft reform with a need for access to higher education institutions by Black students, (2) radical reform or fundamental changes such as decolonisation and (3) beyond-reform which recognises the institution as rooted in violence and unsustainability. We argue that while soft reform has been achieved in many higher education spaces in Africa, the structures and cultures of institutions largely remain reproductions of the colonial past. This despite a significant amount of time being spent initially on debating and theorising decolonisation, what it means and what it could mean for disciplines, and whether or not the different decolonisation movements and theories are the same and if it is thus singular.

1.3 #RhodesMustFall Beyond South Africa: A Global Racial Reckoning?

The imperative to 'decolonise' has become associated with a call to reimagine, transform, and disrupt the role played by universities as sites and producers of knowledge (Bhambra et al. 2018; Jansen 2019). Pennycook and Makoni (2020) argue that it is not only the Global South that is affected by colonisation but also marginalised communities within the Global North. Many of the questions being asked by #RhodesMustFall and #FeesMustFall found parallels in ongoing discourses in education in Europe and North America (see Robertson 2023, which analyses social media posts and shows how student activists created and sustained transnational connections across these interrelated movements). In the current section we highlight and reflect on a limited number of parallel discussions and discourses outside of South Africa, drawing specifically on our experiences in the UK and North America, where two of the authors are based.

In the UK, there have long been calls to address racialised disadvantage in education. Much of this work has focused on higher education with movements such as 'Why is my curriculum white?'—a campaign led by the UK National Union of Students (NUS)—forming part of the broader context. In 2014, the NUS conducted a survey that found that 42% of the respondents did not believe that their curricula reflected issues of diversity, equality and discrimination. The NUS subsequently proposed a set of recommendations, including that institutions "strive to minimise Eurocentric bias in curriculum design, content and delivery and to establish mechanisms to ensure this happens". Universities Scotland also published an example of why and how this can be done via their toolkit 'Embedding Race Equality into the Curriculum'. A number of the NUS campaigns, webinars and events also made direct reference to #RhodesMustFall and movements outside of the UK.

Calls to address racial inequality in UK Higher Education Institutions (HEIs) looked both at issues relating to decolonising the curriculum and to broader issues such as the under-representation of staff from Black, Asian and minoritised backgrounds. In many instances, the focus was on teaching and curricula, with varied responses to the topic, both within and between institutions (Bhambra et al. 2018; Andrews 2020; Gebrial 2020). Again in higher education in particular, there has also been discussion of the so-called awarding gap which sees differences in degree classification along racial lines. On average across the UK, the White versus Black, Asian and minority ethnic 'awarding gap' (the difference in proportions of White and Black, Asian and minority ethnic students awarded a first/2:1 degree) was 9.9% in the academic year 2019/2020 (Advance HE).

The overall 'awarding gap' is primarily driven by gaps in awards of what in the UK are termed 'first-class' degrees—the highest classification of a four-way grade category system. Some 38.9% of White and 28.6% of Black, Asian and minority ethnic students who were included in the statistics were awarded a first-class degree. This represents a gap of 10.2% between the groups. When further disaggregated, White students, on average, received higher awards than students from all other ethnic groups. The awarding gap was particularly pronounced for those from Black African backgrounds (19%), Black Caribbean backgrounds (16.5%) and 'other Black' backgrounds (22.3%) when compared to White qualifiers. Overall, the gap between Black and White graduates was 18.7%. The degree-awarding gap was narrower for Chinese students (2.8%), those who reported 'mixed-ethnicity' (3.9%) and Asian Indian students included in the survey (2.8%). While an in-depth analysis of this situation and the causes for the differences is beyond the scope of the current study, the call in UK higher education to, for example, decolonise the curriculum has often been framed within the larger context of racialised disadvantage, including the 'awarding gap' and other marks of racial inequality.

In 2020, the murder of George Floyd in particular resulted in a renewed sense of urgency and momentum for the Black Lives Matter movement and an increase in global attention to racial inequality. In the UK, this also represented a critical point both in terms of racial awareness and racial justice. This sparked further calls for educational reform which foregrounds racial justice and calls for change which were closely related to decolonial moves, and the development of decolonised curricula. Campaigns such as #RhodesMustFall Oxford was a movement that aimed at "decolonising the space, the curriculum and the institutional memory at, and to fight intersectional oppression within Oxford". Students at Oriel College, University of Oxford also called for the statue of Cecil

Rhodes to be removed from the college, as part of this broader movement. Here we can see even in the name of movement, an explicit acknowledgement of the #RhodesMustFall movement in South Africa. Similarly, 'Leopold Must Fall' (CIGH Exeter 2016; Bhambra et al. 2018: 21) saw a request by student representatives at Queen Mary, University of London to remove plaques commemorating the 1887 visit of King Leopold II of Belgium to the university due to his imperial legacy in Africa, particularly in present-day Democratic Republic of the Congo. Again while these issues are of local importance, their connection to broader global discourses and movements can be seen in both the naming conventions and terminology used, as well as the issues they seek to address—colonialism and its legacy.

Another consequence of the actions in 2020 is that the conversations in the UK spread to different levels of formal education, including primary and secondary school. This resulted in a range of discussions around curriculum reform. People questioned whether what is taught and how it is taught most appropriately reflects both the makeup and diversity of the student body (and society more broadly), and highlighted the limited way in which a range of curricula—history and literature are often singled out for example—fail to engage with the colonial history of the UK.

In the North American context, the murders of George Floyd, Breonna Taylor, and Ahmaud Arbrey, among others, in 2020 set off nationwide and global protests against police violence and (institutional) anti-Blackness in what has been referred to across disciplines and in the public sphere as the "racial reckoning of 2020" (Thomas et al. 2020; Hammonds 2021; Brown and Del Rosso 2022; Burkhard 2022; Clark 2022; Smith 2022; Muehlhausen et al. 2023). Along with being a continuation of the Black Lives Matter movement (Garza 2014), this was coming at a time of disproportionate impacts on Covid-19 on Black and brown communities, as well as increased violence directed at East and South East Asians in the United States (Borja et al. 2020; Ho 2021; Li and Nicholson 2021).

In academia, departments and institutions led efforts to increase the diversity of their faculty, and, in particular, to hire scholars whose work deals with racial justice. Professional organisations also put together responses of various kinds. The Linguistic Society of America put on a series of webinars under the header of "Racial Justice, Equity, Diversity, and Inclusion in the Linguistics Curriculum" (Bucholtz and Soudi 2020; miles-hercules et al. 2020; Namboodiripad and Sanders 2020). The Semantics and Linguistic Theory (SALT) conference established an Equity and Diversity Committee in 2020, and, at their 2021 meeting, put on a workshop on Inclusive Teaching in Semantics (https://saltconf.github.io/salt31/workshop.html). The Ohio State University and the University of Toronto hosted cross-institution workshops on anti-racist/inclusive pedagogy in 2021 and 2022 respectively. These institutions were responding to renewed calls for introspection and action at the level of individuals and institutions, though the events and discussions varied considerably in terms of their scope, goals, and level of engagement with critical perspectives.

Looking back at these efforts, approximately three years later, scholars have come together to critically reflect on their efficacy and impacts. In the context of linguistics in North America, a 2023 workshop at the Linguistic Society of America and a 2023 webinar sponsored by the American Education Research Association's Language and Social Processes Special Interest Group grappled with questions of who did the work, was it effective and what has changed. Critical frameworks such as those of Ahmed (2007, 2012), Calhoun (2021), and Tuck and Yang (2012) which critique neoliberal notions of diversity and decolonisation have been especially helpful for understanding what has gone on. For example, workshop participants noted that there was a focus on linguistic diversity as being a redress to systemic racial inequity, completely bypassing any analyses of power (Calhoun et al. 2023; Muwwakkil et al. 2023). Crucially, much of the work that was done and the critiques of the limitations of institutional responses, were led by junior scholars, such as students and precariously employed researchers/instructors, many of whom came from communities and backgrounds which are historically excluded in the academy.

This is in no way meant as an exhaustive list of actions or responses, rather it reflects on some of the broader context in which this study took place, as well as the work in which we as authors were involved. These movements and our understanding thereof naturally in turn impact our experiences of the issues and our perspectives on the topic. It is against this global backdrop that we four as authors came together and developed the survey to explore the links between African languages and linguistics, and notions of decolonisation and transformation.

In our work as linguists, the pedagogical scope and the tools available to us to address issues of social justice link primarily to the study of language and linguistics. This is the case for research and teaching but are also important considerations our collaborations, citation practices, research methodologies (Chetty et al. 2024) and the underpinning ideas and assumptions on which our research is based (cf. Gibson et al. 2024). Moreover, we consider African languages to be a central part of the path towards decolonisation, the development of decolonised curricula and decolonised universities. This is a notion to which we will return and which is a key theme that emerges in the responses to our survey. It is therefore a natural extension for us to want to explore these ideas and concepts through the confluence of African languages/linguistics and decolonisation and transformation.

1.4 Scope of the Study: What Is African Linguistics?

We framed our survey within the context of African languages and linguistics. A question which a number of our participants asked and grappled with is what we meant to be 'African languages' and 'African linguistics'. In the survey we were not prescriptive about what could be within the scope of the terms 'African languages' and 'African linguistics'. Instead, we left the respondents to interpret these terms as they wished and as would be appropriate in their contexts and areas of work. This is a point we discuss in further detail when outlining the methodology we adopted in Sect. 2.2.3. However, for the purposes of exploring the findings of the survey and for our own conceptualisation of these terms, we wanted to also provide a brief description of what we mean by 'African languages' and 'African linguistics' in the current study.

The way we use the term 'African linguistics' here requires some unpacking and may apply in somewhat different ways to different spaces. In research spaces and journals, African linguistics is relatively clearly defined, based on scholarly practice, and as an areal field. There are journals, several conference series and many books devoted to African linguistics. Most linguists would include in this, the study of languages and linguistic practices located in or recently originating from the African continent. Along with contact languages and signed languages used in Africa and among diasporic communities, this often includes languages that are part of the Niger-Congo and Nilo-Saharan language families, as well as some of the Afro-Asiatic languages, isolates and members of the putative 'Khoisan group.

However, for the purposes of our discussion here, and in the title of this monograph, African Linguistics serves as a shorthand for African linguistics, African languages across higher education spaces and to some extent also linguistics and language classes in Africa (in terms of the space given to African languages in these classes). The aim is to allow us to try to understand the experiences related to African languages and linguistics in a variety of classrooms, including the presence or absence of African languages in language classes for as diverse contexts as French classes in South Africa, Swahili classes in the UK, and general linguistics classes in Malawi or North America.

We did not seek representativeness in the responses we received to the survey, nor to be exhaustive in our questions. The way in which it was administered meant this was not possible (see Sect. 2.2 for further discussion of this). However, we circulated the survey around our networks which, in addition to our contacts in Europe, North America or on the African continent, includes people involved in teaching or learning African languages in Japan, China and Australia. We are aware that the role and positioning of African languages in these contexts may well be different from the contexts in which we are based and which we work in. Our understanding of this term is therefore broad, but also reflected in the responses of our participants, which was in part our intention in carrying out the survey in the first place.

1.5 Structure of the Book

Chapter 1 has presented an introduction to the book, the background to the #RhodesMustFall movement in South Africa and the impact that this and other linked social justice movements have had in recent years internationally. We set out both the background to and the motivation for the online survey and the broader study developed here.

Chapter 2 gives an overview of the methods, and provides some context for interpreting the findings in the subsequent chapters by outlining the overall demographics of the survey respondents. We outline some of the terminology employed in the book, as well as providing some information about us as authors, our positionalities and the contexts in which we are operating.

The subsequent four chapters of the book are structured around the key areas of inquiry that the survey targeted. We were interested in people's experiences of African languages in higher education. This included the experiences of students, the languages they (can) learn, whether they encounter African languages in classes outside of language teaching and linguistics, whether languages are used on campus and the surrounding environments and any other views and experiences in this regard. Similarly, for teaching staff we were interested in the languages they teach, who they teach them to and their broader experiences, both in language/linguistics classes and in other contexts as well.

Chapter 3 explores staff and student experiences of African languages in higher education. We examine the responses to questions which were designed to get a better sense of the prevalence of African language teaching at higher education institutions around the world. In this chapter we also look at the free text responses to a broader question posed in the survey which left respondents open to share any other experiences, thoughts or ideas. We were interested to observe that a large proportion of these responses related to people's broader experiences of African languages in higher education, and so an in-depth exploration of these responses forms the basis of this chapter.

Chapter 4 examines issues related to the incorporation of African languages in higher education, again drawing on the broader discourses as well as the views and experiences of the survey respondents. We were interested in the ways in which African languages were—or were not—embedded into these different spaces and contexts, including beyond language/linguistics classes, for example in history, sociology and economics courses. We were also interested in whether certain African languages are more widely taught and/or used to exemplify specific points. And similarly, whether there are specific (sub-)disciplines which make more widespread use of African languages than others.

Chapter 5 considers respondents' views on the role of African languages and linguistics in decolonisation and transformation in detail, asking how respondents' role in academia and positionalities with regard to African languages shaped their perspectives. We identified some emergent themes in the responses, noting that respondents ranged from feeling that the study of African languages played a central role in decolonisation and transformation to feeling highly sceptical about this idea, and noting that more harm can be done if we assume that simply teaching African languages is the beginning and end of transformation.

Chapter 6 examines respondents' views and attitudes towards decolonisation and transformation more generally. As linguists who are interested in the link between linguistics and social justice, as well as the potential for linguistics to further social justice agendas, we were interested in the way in which people viewed the potential for African languages to be part of a decolonial agenda. This has been a central concern in our own educational and research praxis. And for those of us who are based in Africa, these issues are linked to those at the forefront of discourses in which we are embedded on a daily basis. We were also interested in the similarities and differences in these issues across our locations.

Finally, chap. 7 constitutes a conclusion. Since most of the questions we asked were open-ended, we are interested primarily in the patterns and insights that emerge from the data on which our study is based. This chapter provides us with an opportunity to explore and expand on some of the themes that emerged during the study as well as to highlight ongoing issues, areas for future work and engagement and action in this area.

References

Ahmed, Sara. 2007. 'You end up doing the document rather than doing the doing': Diversity, race equality and the politics of documentation. *Ethnic and Racial Studies* 30: 590–609. https://doi.org/10.1080/01419870701356015.

———. 2012. *On being included: Racism and diversity in institutional life*. Durham: Duke University Press.

Andrews, Kehinde. 2020. The challenge for black studies in the neoliberal university. In *Decolonising the university*, ed. Gurminder K. Bhambra, Kerem Nişancıoğlu, and Dalia Gebrial, 129–144. London: Pluto Press.

Badat, Saleem. 2016a. *Black student politics: Higher education and apartheid from SASO to SANSCO, 1968–1990*. New York: Routledge. https://doi.org/10.4324/9781315829357.

———. 2016b. Deciphering the meanings, and explaining the south African higher education student protests of 2015–16. *Pax Academica* 1 (1): 71–106.

Bhambra, Gurminder K., Kerem Nişancıoğlu, and Dalia Gebrial. 2018. *Decolonising the university*. London: Pluto Press.

Borja, Melissa, Russel Jeung, Aggie Yellow Horse, Jacob Gibson, Sarah Gowing, Nelson Lin, Amelia Navins, and Emahlia Power. 2020. *Anti-Chinese rhetoric tied to racism against Asian Americans stop AAPI hate report*. Asian Pacific Policy & Planning Council.

Breetzke, Gregory D., and David W. Hedding. 2018. The changing demography of academic staff at higher education institutions (HEIs) in South Africa. *Higher Education* 76: 145–161.

Brown, David, and Teri Del Rosso. 2022. Called, committed and inspiring activism: How black PR guest speakers experienced the PR classroom during the COVID-19 and racial reckoning academic year of 2020/2021. *Journal of Public Relations Education* 8 (2): 42–77.

Bucholtz, Mary, and Abdesalam Soudi. 2020. Creating more just and inclusive learning experiences linguistic society of America webinar series: Racial justice, equity, diversity, and inclusion in the linguistics curriculum.

Burkhard, Tanja. 2022. Facing post-truth conspiracies in the classroom. A black feminist autoethnography of teaching for liberation after the summer of racial reckoning. In *Departures in critical qualitative research*, vol. 11, 24–39. University of California Press. https://doi.org/10.1525/dcqr.2022.11.3.24.

Calhoun, Kendra. 2021. *Competing discourses of diversity and inclusion: Institutional rhetoric and graduate student narratives at two minority serving institutions*. UC Santa Barbara, PhD dissertation.

Calhoun, Kendra, Jamaal Muwwakkil, Rachel E. Weissler, Joyhanna Yoo Garza, and Savithry Namboodiripad. 2023. *Linguists' reflections on responses to the 'racial reckoning' of 2020 in U.S. higher education: A collective conversation on lessons learned and next steps presented at the 2023 Linguistic Society of America Annual Meeting*. Boulder, CO.

Cele, G., and C. Koen. 2003. Student politics in South Africa: A study of key developments. *Cahiers de la recherche sur l'éducation et les savoirs* 2: 201–223.

Chetty, Rajendra, Hannah Gibson, and Colin Reilly. 2024. Decolonising methodologies through collaboration: Reflections on partnerships and funding flows from working between the 'south' and the 'north'. In *Decolonizing linguistics*, ed. Anne H. Charity Huddley, Christine Mallinson, and Mary Bucholtz. Oxford: Oxford University Press.

Clark, Brad. Journalism's Racial Reckoning: The News Media's Pivot to Diversity and Inclusion. London: Routledge, 2022. https://doi.org/10.4324/9781003261544.

Council on Higher Education. 2021. *Vital stats: Public higher education 2019*. Pretoria: Council on Higher Education.

Davids, Nuraan, and Yusef Waghid. 2016. History of South African student protests reflects inequality's grip. *The Conversation*. October 9. https://theconversation.com/history-of-south-african-student-protests-reflects-inequalitys-grip-66279.

De Vos, Mark, and Kristina Riedel. 2023. Decolonising and transforming curricula for teaching linguistics and language in South Africa: Taking stock and charting the way forward. *Transformation in Higher Education* 8. https://doi.org/10.4102/the.v8i0.200.

Department of Education. 2001. *National plan for higher education*. Pretoria: Department of Education.

Department of Higher Education and Training. 2013. *White paper for post-school education and training: Building an expanded, effective and integrated post-school system*. Pretoria: Department of Higher Education and Training.

Eberhard, David M., Gary F. Simons, and Charles D. Fennig, eds. 2023. *Ethnologue: Languages of the world*. 26th ed. Dallas, TX: SIL International.

Exeter, CIGH. 2016. Leopold must fall. *Imperial & Global Forum.* https://imperialglobalexeter.com/2016/06/28/leopold-must-fall/. Accessed 30 July 2024.

Falola, Toyin. 2020. The Ibadan School of History. In *From ivory towers to ebony towers transforming humanities curricula in South Africa, Africa and African-American studies,* ed. Oluwaseun Tella and Shireen Motala, 211–227. Johannesburg: Jacana Media.

Garza, Alicia. 2014. A herstory of the #BlackLivesMatter movement. *The Feminist Wire.* October 7.

Gebrial, Dalia. 2020. Rhodes must fall: Oxford and movements for change. In *Decolonising the university,* ed. Gurminder K. Bhambra, Kerem Nişancıoğlu, and Dalia Gebrial. London: Pluto Press.

Gibson, Hannah, Kyle Jerro, Savithry Namboodiripad, and Kristina Riedel. 2024. Towards a decolonial syntax: Research, teaching, publishing. In *Decolonizing linguistics,* ed. Anne H. Charity Hudley, Christine Mallinson, and Mary Bucholtz. Oxford: Oxford University Press.

Govender, Prega. 2016. #FeesMustFall cost 18 varsities more than R460m in damage to property alone. *Mail and Guardian.* October 10. https://mg.co.za/article/2016-09-29-00-feesmustfall-cost-18-varsities-more-than-r460m-in-damage-to-property-alone/.

Güldemann, Tom. 2014. 'Khoisan' linguistic classification today. In *Current issues in linguistic theory,* ed. Tom Güldemann and Anne-Maria Fehn, vol. 330, 1–40. Amsterdam: John Benjamins. https://doi.org/10.1075/cilt.330.01gul.

Hammonds, Evelynn M. 2021. A moment or a movement? The pandemic, political upheaval, and racial reckoning. *Signs: Journal of Women in Culture and Society* 47: 11–14. https://doi.org/10.1086/715650.

Ho, Jennifer. 2021. Anti-Asian racism, black lives matter, and COVID-19. *Japan Forum* 33: 148–159. https://doi.org/10.1080/09555803.2020.1821749.

Jansen, Jonathan D., ed. 2019. *Decolonisation in universities: The politics of knowledge.* Johannesburg: Wits University Press. https://doi.org/10.18772/22019083351.

Jansen, Jonathan D., and Cyrill A. Walters. 2022. *The decolonization of knowledge: Radical ideas and the shaping of institutions in South Africa and beyond.* Cambridge: Cambridge University Press. https://doi.org/10.1017/9781009082723.

Li, Yao, and Harvey L. Nicholson. 2021. When "model minorities" become "yellow peril"—Othering and the racialization of Asian Americans in the COVID-19 pandemic. *Sociology Compass* 15: e12849. https://doi.org/10.1111/soc4.12849.

Mamdani M. Decolonising Universities. In: Jansen J, ed. Decolonisation in Universities: The Politics of Knowledge. Johannesburg: Wits University Press; 2019:15-28.

Maseko, Pamela. 2018. Rethinking Africa series: Whose history counts: Decolonising African pre-colonial historiography. In *Language as source of revitalisation and reclamation of indigenous epistemologies*. Cape Town: Sun Media.

miles-hercules, deandre, Jamaal Muwwakkil, and Kendra Calhoun. 2020. *Racial justice, equity, diversity, and inclusion in the linguistics curriculum: This IS linguistics: Scope, positionality, and graduate apprenticeship when diversifying linguistics curriculum*. Invited talk for a pedagogy webinar put on by the Linguistic Society of America.

Morris, Aldon. 2020. The Atlanta School of Sociology. In *From ivory towers to ebony towers transforming humanities curricula in South Africa, Africa and African-American studies*, ed. Oluwaseun Tella and Shireen Motala, 342–356. Johannesburg: Jacana Media.

Muehlhausen, Beth L., Cate Michelle Desjardins, Beba Shensi Tata-Mbeng, Christa Chappelle, Allison DeLaney, Antonina Olszewski, Csaba Szilagyi, and George Fitchett. 2023. Spiritual care department leaders' response to racial reckoning in 2020 and 2021. *Journal of Health Care Chaplaincy*: 1–15. https://doi.org/10.1080/08854726.2023.2167416.

Muwwakkil, Jamaal, Kendra Calhoun, J. Garza, Savithry Namboodiripad, and R. Weissler. 2023. *Reflections on responses to the 'racial reckoning' of 2020 in U.S. higher education: A collective conversation on lessons learned and next steps*. Webinar sponsored by the American Education Research Association Language and Social Processes Special Interest Group. Online.

Namboodiripad, Savithry, and Nathan Sanders. 2020. *Centering linguistic diversity and justice in course design*. Presented at the Linguistic Society of America webinar series: Racial Justice, Equity, Diversity, and Inclusion in the Linguistics Curriculum. August 14.

Ngũgĩ wa Thiong'o. 1986. *Decolonising the mind: The politics of language in African literature*. London: James Currey.

Pennycook, Alastair, and Sinfre Makoni. 2020. *Innovations and challenges in applied linguistics from the global south*. London: Routledge.

Reddy, Thiven. 2004. *Higher education and social transformation: South Africa case study*. Johannesburg: Council for Higher Education.

Robertson, Rebecca. 2023. A critical race theory analysis of transnational student activism, social media counter-stories, and the hegemonic logics of diversity work in higher education. *International Journal of Qualitative Studies in Education* 36: 900–917. https://doi.org/10.1080/09518398.2021.1885073.

Smith, Patriann. 2022. Black immigrants in the United States: Transraciolinguistic justice for imagined futures in a global metaverse. *Annual Review of Applied Linguistics* 42: 109–118. https://doi.org/10.1017/S0267190522000046.

Thomas, Kevin D., Judy Foster Davis, Jonathan A.J. Wilson, and Francesca Sobande. 2020. Repetition or reckoning: Confronting racism and racial dynamics in 2020. *Journal of Marketing Management* 36: 1153–1168. Routledge. https://doi.org/10.1080/0267257X.2020.1850077.

Tuck, Eve, and K. Wayne Yang. 2012. Decolonization is not a metaphor. *Decolonization: Indigeneity, Education & Society* 1: 1–40.

Universities South Africa. 2015. *Reflections on higher education transformation discussion paper*. Prepared for the second national Higher Education Transformation Summit.

Witzlack-Makarevich, Alena, and Hirosi Nakagawa. 2019. Linguistic features and typologies in languages commonly referred to as 'Khoisan'. In *The Cambridge handbook of African linguistics*, ed. H. Ekkehard Wolff, 382–416. Cambridge: Cambridge University Press. https://doi.org/10.1017/9781108283991.012.

Zembylas, Michalinos. 2018. Decolonial possibilities in south African higher education: Reconfiguring humanising pedagogies as/with decolonising pedagogies. *South African Journal of Education* 38: 1–11. https://doi.org/10.15700/saje.v38n4a1699.

Open Access This chapter is licensed under the terms of the Creative Commons Attribution 4.0 International License (http://creativecommons.org/licenses/by/4.0/), which permits use, sharing, adaptation, distribution and reproduction in any medium or format, as long as you give appropriate credit to the original author(s) and the source, provide a link to the Creative Commons license and indicate if changes were made.

The images or other third party material in this chapter are included in the chapter's Creative Commons license, unless indicated otherwise in a credit line to the material. If material is not included in the chapter's Creative Commons license and your intended use is not permitted by statutory regulation or exceeds the permitted use, you will need to obtain permission directly from the copyright holder.

CHAPTER 2

The Survey, the Respondents and Us

Abstract This chapter gives an overview of the methods used for the survey on which the study is based. This includes a description of how the survey was administered and distributed. We then provide context for interpreting the findings in the subsequent chapters by outlining the overall demographics of the survey respondents, defining some of the terminology employed in the book, as well as providing some information about us as authors, our positionalities and the contexts in which we are operating.

Keywords Methods • Survey • Location • Demographics • Respondents • Participants

2.1 Overview

The survey on which the current study is based was administered online using the online survey software Qualtrics. Responses to the survey were collected between January and June 2021. The survey was completed anonymously, and we made sure not to collect any identifying information, including IP addresses or location. We sought and received ethical approval from each institution, including Nelson Mandela University (H20-HUM-ALS-EAP-002), University of the Free State (UFS-HSD2020/0087/3108), and University of Essex (ETH1920-1802); the

© The Author(s) 2025
H. Gibson et al., *African Linguistics after #RhodesMustFall*,
https://doi.org/10.1007/978-3-031-74817-2_2

survey methods were submitted to the Institutional Review Board at the University of Michigan (HUM00187703) and declared "exempt".

We did not limit the responses to particular locations in order to be able to capture the potentially global impacts of these discourses, including crucially both within and outside Africa. We wrote the following short message in our recruitment messages, which was also included in the description of the survey itself:

> We are interested in people's experiences of African languages in higher education settings, particularly in linguistics and language classes. This includes your own experiences of using African languages at home or in the community, as well as your experiences of African languages at university. We are keen to hear from students and teachers, as well as those who might be both!

We intended to cast as wide a net as possible in terms of potential degree of engagement with African languages. We did not have any limitations on participants based on geography or stage in academia. We distributed the survey via our own personal and professional networks, and subject area mailing lists, such as the LinguistList, LingType listserv, Teaching Linguistics LSA Special Interest Group, Committee for Ethnic Diversity in Linguistics LSA Special Interest Group, LingAnth listserv, CUNY sentence processing listserv, SLE, FunkNet, Linguistics Association of Great Britain forum, British Association of Applied Linguistics Africa Special Interest Group, Southern African Linguistics and Applied Linguistics Society (SALALS) newsletter, as well as via Facebook for the SALALS group and the African language documentation group. We also shared the survey on the platform Twitter (now X).

Before participants were asked for their consent and given the option to begin the survey, we described ourselves, the research team, giving our names and affiliations and saying "We are an international group of researchers who are interested in experiences of and thoughts on decolonisation/transformation and social justice in higher education, in particular we are interested in how these relate to African languages." We also informed potential participants that we intended to present the results of the survey at conferences and to develop an academic publication based on the findings.

The survey comprised 26 questions covering biographical information, experiences with and exposure to African languages both outside of formal education and in higher education institutions in general, as well as questions relating to attitudes to African languages and linguistics, and notions of decolonisation and transformation (see Appendix for a full list of the survey questions). We estimated that the survey would take 10–20 minutes to complete, although in practice there was significant variation in completion times, as participants could start and stop at any point. If the survey lay idle for two weeks, the partial responses were submitted automatically. We received 268 responses to the survey. Responses with a completion rate below 3% were removed and we worked with the remaining 181 responses. Participants could skip any questions, so the number of responses for most of the questions discussed here is under 181.

In almost all cases, questions were open-ended, so that participants could respond as relevant to their own contexts, and in as much detail as they would like. For a limited number of questions we asked for yes/no answers. For social categories such as role in academia, race/ethnicity, and gender, we did not want to impose external labels which might not be relevant for all respondents' local contexts. As such, we left these categories open-ended and then in some cases, as part of our analysis we did a round of coding to make the open-ended responses comparable across the respondents. We describe and motivate this below and in subsequent chapters as relevant.

2.2 About the Respondents

2.2.1 Respondents by Location

The survey was open to anyone who wished to complete it. However we note some inherent biases in the data gathered. Two of the four of us are based in Africa, and three of the four of us specifically work on or within African languages and linguistics. As a result, our professional networks also reflect this and are skewed towards those with similar areas of interest, expertise or who are based in or have links with Africa.

Similarly, it is likely that people who are already interested in African languages and linguistics were more likely to complete the survey. Similarly, those who are based in Africa—including with no link to language and linguistics—completed the survey at a higher rate than those outside of Africa. Finally, since we also explicitly mentioned decolonisation and transformation in the description of the survey, it is also likely that those with

Fig. 2.1 A visualisation of where survey respondents were based; size of circle represents frequency

some degree of interest in these issues were more likely to complete the survey, meaning that our responses again reflect this.

To understand more about how our networks might have had an impact on responses, and, crucially, because we expect that location would be a relevant factor in shaping our participants' experiences, we asked for participants' current location as well as all of the countries where they have spent a significant amount of time across their lives. This is illustrated in Fig. 2.1 which shows where our respondents indicated they were based, with the size of the circle corresponding to the relative number of respondents who selected a particular country.

While we had a small number of responses from Asia and Australia, we received no responses from South America or the Caribbean. Responses from Europe and North America are over-represented from a comparative perspective. Similarly, within the African context, South Africa is overrepresented, as are a few specific locations in Eastern Africa—specifically, Tanzania and Kenya. We also had responses from Nigeria and Cameroon, but we noted the absence of responses from other parts of Western Africa and North Africa. Looking just at respondents located in Africa versus those outside of Africa, about 46% were located in Africa ($N = 82$), and 54% elsewhere ($N = 97$).

Again, responses were open-ended, so we aggregated into very general regions in order to get a picture of our participants' current locations, as seen in Table 2.1. Three respondents indicated that they split their time equally between two regions, which we did capture in the broad categorisation in Table 2.1 (n.b., this is not captured in the map in Fig. 2.1; we arbitrarily chose the first location that participants wrote to make the map).

Table 2.1 Participants' current location, coded for uniformity based on open-ended responses

	Participants' current location
Africa	81 (45%)
Europe	69 (39%)
North America	21 (12%)
Asia	3 (2%)
Australasia	1 (>1%)
Australia	1 (>1%)
Europe/Africa	1 (>1%)
Europe/Asia	1 (>1%)
North America/Europe	1 (>1%)
Total	179

We expected that not only would current location be relevant, but also that experiences of mobility—very common amongst students and academics—would be potentially relevant. For example, those who grew up in Asia but now live and work in North America likely have different frames for understanding and experiencing colonialism than those who spent the majority of their lives and careers in North America. We did not have enough participants who gave us sufficient detail to say much more about this, but we will include that information if it is relevant to our discussions of particular participants' responses.

2.2.2 Respondents by Role in Academia

Because a major goal of this study was to understand how African languages are integrated (or not) in academic contexts, as well as to understand how our participants experienced these student movements and related movements for decolonisation, transformation, and racial justice, it was relevant to us to know what stage in academia our participants were in.

In terms of other broad characteristics, respondents comprised students and instructors; 56 of the respondents indicated that they were undergraduate students and 41 postgraduate students. The survey was completed by 11 who indicated that they were postdoctoral researchers. We received 3 responses from adjunct faculty, 27 responses from Assistant Professors, 11 from Associate Professors, 9 from Professors, 1 Emeritus Professor, 2 Research Assistants. 4 respondents indicated that they were Alt-ac (employed in non-academic fields), 3 marked teacher and 11 marked 'other'.

However, because many of our research questions centred around differing experiences of those preparing and delivering lessons versus those who receive instruction, we did a round of coding which created five categories, as seen in Table 2.2. This was determined not just based on combining the more fine-grained categories, but we looked across to other questions about whether participants had taught, as well as their highest degree, in order to better determine their relationship to delivering instruction.

Faculty represent the biggest proportion of respondents overall. Faculty were assumed to be mainly responding with their experience of preparing lessons in mind, though they have all been students themselves of course— this included postdoctoral scholars, emeritus professors and non-tenure-stream instructors. We recognise that not all of these roles mean that the respondents are currently preparing lessons or teaching themselves, but, based on their responses, we could determine that they had done so at least at some point recently. Graduate students are often preparing lessons and receiving lessons simultaneously, and even though some may be in programmes which do not include teaching opportunities, we wanted to separate them out as they certainly have a different relationship to academic engagement as compared to undergraduates and faculty. MA and PhD students were grouped together for this broad categorisation. Undergraduate students, assumed to be primarily recipients of lessons, were the most under-represented in this survey, as they are the biggest constituency in academia and yet only the second-largest group of respondents. The category of 'Other' was used to capture those not on the academic track, who we could not determine if they had prepared or will prepare lessons themselves, and Q represents participants whose role we could not determine.

As evidenced from Table 2.2, faculty represent the biggest proportion of respondents, followed by undergraduates and then graduate students. As with the location of participants, this is explained by our own networks and also who is likely to come across and complete such a survey. While some of our faculty colleagues distributed this survey to their students, we did not ask for this to happen systematically, and therefore faculty are overrepresented amongst our respondents.

However, we also noticed a strong skew in terms of location and role in academia amongst our participants when we split our responses based on

2 THE SURVEY, THE RESPONDENTS AND US   29

Table 2.2 Participants' role in academia

	Participants' current role in academia
Faculty	73 (40%)
Graduate	41 (23%)
Undergraduate	56 (31%)
Other	10 (6%)
Q	1 (>1%)
Total	181

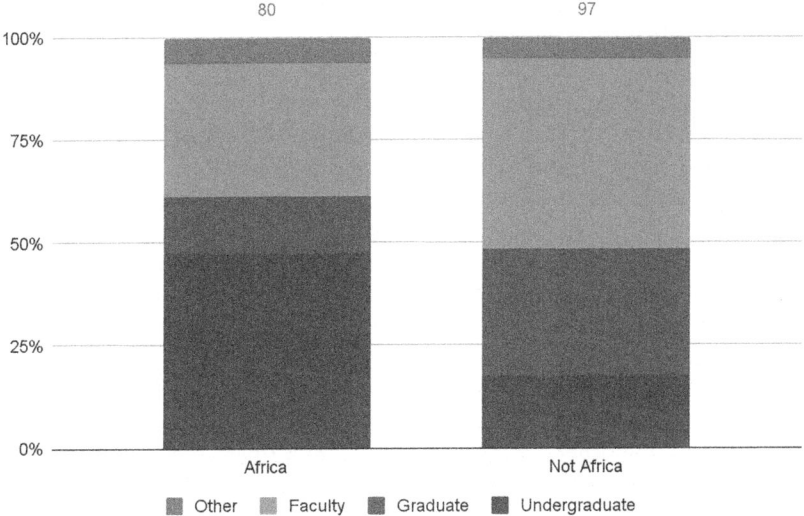

Fig. 2.2 Stacked bar plot of participants' role in academia based on whether or not they are located in Africa

whether participants were currently located in Africa or not. Our undergraduate respondents were much more likely to be located in Africa, and, indeed, as shown in the stacked bar plot in Fig. 2.2, almost half of our respondents who are located in Africa were undergraduates ($N = 38$), as opposed to less than 20% of all participants located outside of Africa ($N = 17$). As such, any generalisation which emerges about location or role in academia alone should be interpreted with this additional bias in mind.

A note on terminology is required here. We use the terms *faculty* and *staff* interchangeably here to mean employees who participate in instructional roles in higher education. Employees who do not participate in instruction are designated *other*. This departs from how these terms are in the context of the United States higher education, where *faculty* and *staff* are often distinguished, with staff being administrators and other non-instructional employees, and faculty being instructional employees. However, as our survey was completed by respondents from outside the United States and these terms are used interchangeably elsewhere, we follow that convention.

2.2.3 Respondent's Gender and Race/Ethnicity

Along with location and academic role, we asked about two main social categories—race/ethnicity and gender. We asked about these both in open-ended ways: "How would you describe yourself in terms of race/ethnicity?" and "I identify my gender as ...", with a short response box presented under each. We did not have explicit hypotheses about how gender might inform experiences of studying African languages and perspectives on decolonisation/transformation movements in academic contexts, and we ended up not using that information in our analyses or interpretations in this book.

However, as seen in Table 2.3, we did have overwhelmingly more responses from participants who self-identified as women or female as compared to any other group. Note that the "Other" category here represented responses which were rejecting the premise of asking about gender by not directly answering the question; these could have also been grouped with "prefer not to respond", which is what that participant

Table 2.3 Participants' self-reported gender, aggregated based on open-ended responses

	Participants' self-reported gender
Woman/Female	119 (66%)
Man/Male	51 (28%)
Agender/Nonbinary/Genderqueer	8 (4%)
Other	2 (1%)
Prefer not to respond	1 (>1%)
Total	181

wrote. Participants whose gender identities do not fall into the binary were grouped together in the "Agender/Nonbinary/Genderqueer" category, which we labelled based on the terms used by respondents themselves.

Since racial labels in particular are colonial products, we assumed that participants' experiences of being racialised would be important to understanding their perspectives on transformation and/or decolonisation, which is why we asked participants to tell us how they self-identified in terms of race/ethnicity. We intentionally included race and ethnicity in the same open-ended question, as this allowed participants to conflate or separate the two in whichever way felt relevant to them without us having to give a long description of the various distinctions. As such, the terminology used in this study has been selected to align with each participant's response to the open-ended question: "*How would you describe yourself in terms of race/ethnicity?*"

Some participants wrote "African" or "mixed", while others listed a more specific ethnic identity, such as Cape Malay, Berber or German. Note that some participants based in South Africa used the term "coloured", an emic term for those who are mixed race of various backgrounds and we use this term where relevant when describing participants who self-identified that way. In Table 2.4, which gives a snapshot of the way our participants described their race/ethnicity (we included "coloured" under the heading "bi/multiracial" for the purposes of this table).

Racial and ethnic labels cannot be understood without both global and local contextualisation. Because we assumed that participants would have

Table 2.4 Participants' self-reported race/ethnicity, aggregated based on open-ended responses

	Participants' self-reported race (aggregated)
White	79 (51%)
Black	36 (23%%)
Bi/multiracial	11 (7%%)
Asian	9 (6%)
European	8 (5%)
African diaspora	5 (3%)
West Asian/North African	3 (2%)
No response	2 (1%)
Asian diaspora	1 (>1%)
Total	154

approached the way that they self-identify in very different ways (given the variation in responses, that assumption seems to have been founded), we do not include these labels as part of any rudimentary quantitative analysis. Instead, we include this information, when it was given, as part of how we describe a participant, alongside their location and role in academia, for example. Crucially, we do slightly generalise the labels in some cases to preserve anonymity; if the participant wrote "Pakistani" for example, we might write "South Asian" instead in order to not single out a Pakistani faculty member in Australia, to take a constructed example. However, care has been taken throughout to align these labels as closely as possible to how participants self-described.

In terms of terminology, we have opted to capitalise Black throughout when used to refer to race, acknowledging still that this is a construct. There is also ongoing discussion relating to the capitalisation of 'White' to show that this is also a construct and to highlight the way in which Whiteness functions, we have opted here to also capitalise White in order to highlight the constructed nature of this category as well, following discussions such as the Diversity Style Guide entry "white, White" (Kanigel 2016).

2.2.4 Respondents' Language Background

Along with asking about respondents' experiences of teaching or learning African languages, which were questions we discuss in more detail in Chaps. 3 and 4, we also asked respondents whether they grew up speaking an African language or languages, and if African languages were used in their home or surrounding areas where they grew up. There was an approximately half/half split for the former question, with 47% of respondents (N = 85) saying that 'Yes' they grew up speaking an African language and 53% (N = 96) responding 'No'. As for whether African languages were used in the home or in surrounding areas, 54% (N = 97) said 'Yes', that African languages were spoken either in their home or surrounding areas, 45% (N = 82) said 'No', and there were two participants who gave no response.

A note here is necessary in terms of the notion of 'African languages' (cf. Sect. 1.4 where we touch on this question in relation to asking what constitutes African linguistics). In pre-distribution feedback we received on the survey, a number of people asked exactly what we meant by the term 'African languages'. Did we mean Arabic? Was French included?

What about Afrikaans where its grouping in terms of language family is distinct from its geographic location? Were we only interested in languages spoken in certain parts of the continent or from certain language families? We deliberately left this open to be interpreted by respondents as they chose but we note that this might have been interpreted differently amongst the respondents. Participants' own responses to these questions sometimes grappled with this, but they more often specified "South African English", "Moroccan Arabic", or something similar to indicate that they considered those languages to be African. From the specific mentions of African languages, many participants broadly construed the term as including signed languages, creoles and African varieties of former colonial languages. These responses and the patterns we identified in this regard are discussed in Chap. 4.

Most of the questions we asked were open-ended, and, as such, any sort of generalisations or summaries of the responses given here are based on our secondary coding and interpretation. Further, our claims and observations here are not based on any perceived idea of representativeness nor exhaustiveness. Rather, we are interested in insights and patterns that did emerge from the observed data. Taken together, this approach to data collection and survey construction was more conducive to qualitative rather than quantitative analyses, and that is what comprises the majority of the findings in this book.

2.3 Who We Are, Our Positionalities and the Contexts in Which We Are Based

We write as academics working in different contexts and as individuals with different positionalities. We are variously based in the UK, South Africa and the United States, and bring together different disciplinary interests, expertise and experiences. We provide further detail on our own backgrounds, experiences, positionalities and broader higher education contexts below. However, here we want to briefly mention why we believe this is relevant—and important—information to include and how this links to and influences the study, how we carried it out and what we were interested in learning. As such, descriptions of our perspectives are central to descriptions of our methods.

Recent years have seen an increase in calls for researchers to include information on their own positionality in their work. This is often presented under the title of 'positionality statements'. As also noted by others, these may be written as 'confessionals' (Pillow 2003), as disclosures of researcher identities (Secules et al. 2021), or in order to justify authority through naming professional proximity to marginalised groups (Boveda and Annamma 2023). Boveda and Annamma (2023) also warn against simply making statements and not fully understanding the power and function of positioning in order to write these statements in a meaningful way.

Below we include information about our positionalities and the contexts in which we operate as the four authors of this monograph. We include what are essentially our academic biographies, the primary areas of our research and teaching, and how we came to work on issues of decolonisation and transformation in higher education. However, we also include information about us as individuals and our identities. We believe that our positionalities as researchers are relevant for the current study, for our initial interest in this topic in the first place, for the questions we asked, our interpretation of the data and for the conclusions we reached. We have therefore included this information here, as part of how we describe and contextualise our methods.

Hannah Gibson is Professor of Linguistics at the University of Essex in the UK. Most of her research relates to African languages, this includes work on morphosyntactic variation in the Bantu languages of Eastern and Southern Africa, as well as work examining the impact of language policy in multilingual contexts. Hannah grew up in the UK with a mixed Black Caribbean and White English background. Part of her involvement in work on decolonising the curriculum and seeking to address racial inequality in higher education come from her experience as Black academic where she has found herself both invisible and hypervisible. Her own experiences of formal education contribute to the imperative she feels to be involved in work to address racialised disadvantage in education. This, combined with her research focus on African languages, have given rise to some of the work she has been involved in on decolonising the curriculum, decolonising research and raising the profile of African languages both at her own institution and in linguistics more widely.

In terms of discipline-specific contributions, Hannah co-founded the Linguistics Association of Great Britain's (LAGB) race and social justice committee in 2020. She has also been involved in collaborations with colleagues at the University of the Western Cape in South Africa looking at the links between decolonisation, transformation and language and linguistics. In recent collaborative work, including with Savithry and Kristina, she has also co-authored a chapter in the edited volume *Decolonizing Linguistics* (Charity-Hudley et al. 2024) entitled 'Towards a decolonial syntax: Research, teaching, publishing', as well as a chapter with Rajendra Chetty and Colin Reilly entitled 'Decolonising methodologies through collaboration: reflections on partnerships and funding flows from working between the "South" and the "North"' in the same volume.

Jacqueline Lück currently is a Senior Lecturer in the Department of Linguistics and Applied Linguistics as well as the Deputy Dean in the Faculty of Humanities at Nelson Mandela University. Her research includes a focus on inclusion of students into disciplinary knowledge and how language constrains or enables this. Her teaching interests are in Sociolinguistics and Psycholinguistics. Her research interests are language, knowledge and curriculum; identity, discourse and ideology; decolonisation of linguistics and decolonisation of the curriculum. She was part of a National Research Foundation project that looks at how knowledge includes or excludes students in higher education. She also works closely with the university's teaching and learning community in their quest to decolonise and Africanise curriculum and language policy. She serves on a number of institutional committees that include the Decolonisation Working Group, the Equality Group and First Nations Group—with a focus on restoration of Khoekhoegowab in the Eastern Cape.

Jacqueline came to this project after a long career in education and sees herself as being deeply concerned with issues of equity and access, redress and reclamation in education and in civil society. She grew up in apartheid South Africa and so the issues of this monograph concern her greatly. She was classified as "Coloured" in terms of apartheid racial descriptors and grew up in areas and went to schools designated for South Africans of mixed racial background. She experienced first-hand the impact of the Group Areas Act (or forced removals) and other apartheid laws on communities and has engaged in political activism since her teens. Outside of academia, she continues to work closely with civil society structures, schools, frail care centres, women mentorship and women at risk programmes in impoverished communities. She is interested to see how inclusive or not global language academic spaces are. She is intentional about the foregrounding of all knowledges in both her academic work and scholarly writings.

Savithry Namboodiripad is Assistant Professor in Linguistics at the University of Michigan, Ann Arbor. Her research uses experimental methods to study syntactic typology and language contact, as well as asking how methodological and theoretical approaches might need to be shifted in order to do such work. Along with the joint work on *Decolonising Syntax* described above, she has worked with collaborators interrogating the utility of essentialist constructs such as *native speaker* and *competence* in linguistic theory and practice. She has been involved in the Linguistic Society of America's Committee on Ethnic Diversity in Linguistics, most recently as co-chair, has co-organised a workshop and working group on Equity, Diversity and Inclusion in Language Evolution, and is currently co-leading a group working towards moving past essentialist notions of identity and language in institutional contexts (https://rolecollective. org/). Unlike the other co-authors of this monograph, her research does not focus on African languages, but rather engages with colonialism and globalisation via studies of language contact between Malayalam and English in Kerala, India and amongst diaspora populations in North America.

Savithry is a South Asian-American woman who grew up in the United States speaking Malayalam and English. Her family are Namboodiris, part of a traditionally landowning community in Kerala, India; as such, she has caste privilege, and the relationship between Namboodiris and the surrounding communities in Kerala can be viewed through a colonial frame. Due to the volatile and revocable nature of caste and its dependence on adherence to community norms, her personal relationship to that privilege is in some contexts revoked and plays a variable role in interactions in research contexts. Her research participants and interlocutors often experience language oppression and shift due to globalisation and assimilationist contexts; this is also relevant to her own experience growing up as a racialised bilingual in a predominantly White monolingual American community. In her reflection and writing on colonialism, the oppressive context of her cultural background and her position as an academic in the United States shape the types of questions she asks and hegemonies she seeks to disrupt. These overlapping commitments, along with her previous experience using survey methodology to ask about harassment and bias in linguistics (Namboodiripad et al. 2019), are what led her to be part of this project.

Kristina Riedel is Senior Lecturer in Linguistics at the University of the Witwatersrand in Johannesburg, South Africa. She has been in this post since mid-2023, after spending more than seven years working as Senior Lecturer at the University of the Free State (UFS) in Bloemfontein, South Africa. Her research is focused on the morphosyntax of Bantu languages, especially those of South Africa and East Africa. Her teaching interests centre on African languages broadly, as well as general and theoretical linguistics. As noted above, she has collaborated with Hannah and Savithry on 'Decolonising Syntax' (Gibson et al. 2024). She has also recently published a co-authored paper on perceptions of and approaches to transformation and decolonisation by language academics in South Africa (de Vos and Riedel 2023). This study was based on a workshop presentation on decolonisation at Nelson Mandela University, where she also met Jacqueline which led to them working together within various academic fora and developing the study for this monograph together.

Kristina was born and raised in Berlin, Germany, in a White, middle-class family. She studied Swahili and Linguistics at SOAS University of London, before obtaining a PhD at Leiden University and working at the University of Illinois at Urbana-Champaign as a non-tenure track faculty member teaching Swahili. She has also spent a significant amount of time in Tanzania as a student and researcher. The colonial and present histories, cultures, and social and geographical settings of these places have formed her thinking about higher education. The #RhodesMustFall protests began while Kristina was preparing her move to South Africa from the University of Illinois at Urbana-Champaign and this shaped her first years as an academic in South Africa. She was involved in founding a RhodesMustFall-inspired staff group at UFS and the various Southern African Applied Linguistics Association and Linguistics Society of Southern Africa workshops on transformation and decolonisation of Linguistics in South Africa, one of which she hosted. While at the University of Illinois, Kristina was involved in forming a union of non-tenure track faculty and an active member of the wider campus labour movement. Her involvement in the current project grew from these efforts and conversations with colleagues.

There are parallels between the locations we inhabit and in many ways this is what has drawn us to work jointly on this project. However, there are also important differences with respect to African languages and the notions of decolonisation and transformation. Hannah is based in the UK which has a long history of colonisation both within its own shores and internationally. The UK has in many ways continued to fail to engage fully with its colonial past, as well as the ways in which the impacts of this are still felt today. There is ongoing work in higher education to address racialised disadvantage, to develop decolonised curricula and to acknowledge the UK's imperialist past and present. In the UK, notions of decolonisation typically link directly to the UK's history of settler-colonialism and imperial rule. There was a widespread and long-lasting British colonial presence across much of Africa and indeed globally. The position and role of the UK in broader systems of violence such as slavery and imperial systems of oppression and exploitation are also central to this debate.

In terms of higher education, the UK is a popular destination for students from across the world. However, while the UK student body is increasingly racially diverse—both in terms of global appeal and in terms of the racial makeup of students from the UK—this is in many instances not reflected in the makeup of staff/faculty and the slow pace of change in this regard has also formed part of discourses on decolonisation—and diversification—of the UK educational landscape. In the UK, there has traditionally been limited discourse on issues such as reparations and discourses on land for example do not play a central part in these discussions (in contrast to the situation in the United States for example).

Savithry is based in the United States, where decolonisation is mainly centred around the work of Native American, Native Hawaiian, and Puerto Rican activists and scholars, though the role of the United States in the Philippines and harmful global interventions via the military and/ or non-governmental organisations which amount to neocolonialism are given critique as well. Overall, any meaningful or material remunerations for the colonialist past and present of the United States are practically non-existent, and there is little public awareness or movement for doing so (cf. movements for slavery reparations and giving land back to Black citizens whose property was stolen due to racist practices —such policies have been highly limited regionally, but have gained some more momentum in recent years). The University of Michigan and other "land grant" institutions have been and are implicated in the settler colonial project. While various actions have been taken to think about renaming buildings and giving back "artefacts" stolen from indigenous nations and Global South contexts, ongoing actions which can be framed in a (neo-)colonial way, have received criticism (Nash 2019; Stein 2020; Garton 2021).

Jacqueline and Kristina are both based in South Africa and therefore operating from within an African context. About a third of the survey respondents reported being based in South Africa and this is reflected in many of their answers and their approaches to the concepts we were interested in and which we discuss below. This includes the participants' view on which languages are featured in classes or discussed in this context, the types of courses offered and the overall perspectives on higher education. Importantly, there are discourses in the South African context on issues relating to decolonisation and transformation with transformation having been the main reference term since the end of apartheid. But during and after #RhodesMustFall the term decolonisation has also featured prominently. Decolonisation concerns are with the transformation of the academy in terms of demographics, as well as the canon of knowledge. The focus is on strengthening an Africa-centred curriculum towards epistemic access with the nature of the knowledge coming under interrogation. Pressing and ongoing issues in the South African higher education relate to student funding and related aspects of student life such as housing and personal safety, success rates, staff demographics, campus culture and language use, in particular the fact that despite the vast majority of South African speaking one or more Bantu languages, universities, apart from language classes and a small number of subjects (especially education), only use English (and in very few public higher education settings also Afrikaans) as medium of instruction, and curricula and resources are not focused on the local or African setting or students' lived experiences.

To be able to follow the discussions in the subsequent chapter, we think a brief overview of the linguistic situation in South Africa, as far as it pertains to language use in higher education, may be helpful for readers who are not familiar with this context. Prior to transition to democracy, English and Afrikaans were already recognised as national languages in the country. Upon transition to democracy, nine Bantu languages were added as national languages: Ndebele and Sepedi (Northern Sotho), Sesotho (Southern Sotho), Swati, Tsonga, Tswana, Venda, Xhosa and Zulu. In 2023, South African Sign Language was added as an official language. Despite the increased recognition for a wider range of languages, and particularly African languages, many of the apartheid era's linguistic categorisations and practices were retained. This included for example the rigid and directive/legislative approach towards first and second languages, a narrow focus by institutions on just one or two African languages, not only in terms of use in institutional communications and as medium of instruction but also as languages taught. Moreover, as noted frequently, the number of official languages from the Bantu language group often seems to be used as an excuse to avoid rather than further their use in different government and educational settings.

In South Africa, Bantu languages are used as a medium of instruction for the first years of primary school but not in secondary or tertiary education, beyond the courses on those languages. There are also no attempts to or discussions about accommodating the languages of significant migrant and minority groups in South Africa. There are plans for example to introduce Swahili instruction in schools, despite the fact that it is not taught at degree level at any South African university, nor is it spoken in South Africa except as a language of relatively small groups of migrants or heritage language speakers. It is therefore not clear how South African school teachers are expected to acquire relevant skills for teaching Swahili to students. We reflect on these issues and attitudes below, especially in Chaps. 3 and 4.

In the South African academic context, the term 'transformation' is used widely (see Sect. 1.2 for a definition and further discussion). As noted above, while this overlaps with decolonisation, it is also typically seen as broader in terms of seeking to address racial, social and economic injustices from the apartheid past and their repercussions on South African society today. It is also important to note that the specific context at South African institutions of higher learning differs significantly as influenced by factors such as being formerly White institutions or historically Black universities, the present or former medium of instructions as English or Afrikaans and those institutional histories whose self-perception was more in opposition or more in alignment with apartheid ideologies. Universities also differ in terms of their student and staff demographics in terms of race which remains rather strongly linked to language and linguistic expertise, and to some extent also in terms of having international staff and students. While the most prestigious universities still have predominantly White staff members and administrators this is not the case for HBIs and this affected how the student movements played out, despite the fact that these types of institutions and their institutional cultures are also in need of transformation and decolonisation.

Jansen and Walters (2022: 12) describe the difference in the focus of the student movements at HBIs as follows:

> the felt need for decolonization was less emphatically expressed at the historically Black universities, in part because the major agitations among disadvantaged institutions were material rather than ideological, concerned with the bread-and-butter issues better represented by the #FeesMustFall movement. These universities, too, at least in their student enrolments and cultures, were more distinctively Black than institutions such as the University of Cape Town.

As scholars working in these three contexts, we draw on our own perspectives as well as our experiences of our involvement in the work that is being done in these three locations. We are aware of the need for context-specific responses to these challenges, as well as the strength that comes from forging international allegiances and collaborations. We are also aware that in many ways, the issues we discuss here in relation to knowledge production transcend national boundaries. We explore issues of marginalisation and erasure of African languages, issues of salience, as well as attitudes towards African languages, all of which are linked to and embedded in the contexts in which they are found and expressed. We also explore issues of empowerment, decolonisation, transformation and reform, which again are viewed differently in our respective contexts. It is our belief however that through combining these distinct, yet interconnected, insights, we can better understand the positioning of African languages in higher education, and ultimately the link between African languages and the decolonial turn.

In the next chapter we explore student and staff experiences of African languages in higher education, drawing on responses to the survey and key themes and patterns that emerged.

REFERENCES

Boveda, Mildred, and Subini Ancy Annamma. 2023. Beyond making a statement: An intersectional framing of the power and possibilities of positioning. *Educational Researcher*. https://doi.org/10.3102/0013189X231167149.

Charity-Huddley, Anne H., Christine Mallinson, and Mary Bucholtz, eds. 2024. *Decolonising Linguistics*. Oxford: Oxford University Press.

De Vos, Mark, and Kristina Riedel. 2023. Decolonising and transforming curricula for teaching linguistics and language in South Africa: Taking stock and charting the way forward. *Transformation in Higher Education* 8. https://doi.org/10.4102/the.v8i0.200.

Garton, Paul. 2021. Types of anchor institution initiatives: An overview of university urban development literature. *Metropolitan Universities* 33: 85–105. https://doi.org/10.18060/25242.

Gibson, Hannah, Kyle Jerro, Savithry Namboodiripad, and Kristina Riedel. 2024. Towards a decolonial syntax: Research, teaching, publishing. In *Decolonizing linguistics*, ed. Anne H. Charity Hudley, Christine Mallinson, and Mary Bucholtz. Oxford: Oxford University Press.

Jansen, Jonathan D., and Cyrill A. Walters. 2022. *The decolonization of knowledge: Radical ideas and the shaping of institutions in South Africa and beyond.*

Cambridge: Cambridge University Press. https://doi.org/10.1017/97810 09082723.

Kanigel, Rachele. 2016. White, white. *Diversity Style Guide*. April 12.

Namboodiripad, Savithry, Corrine Occhino, and Lynn Hou. 2019. *A survey of linguists and language researchers: Harassment, bias, and what we can do about it*. Plenary panel presented at the 93rd Annual Meeting of the Linguistic Society of America, New York City.

Nash, Margaret A. 2019. Entangled pasts: Land-Grant colleges and American Indian dispossession. *History of Education Quarterly* 59: 437–467. Cambridge University Press. https://doi.org/10.1017/heq.2019.31.

Pillow, Wanda. 2003. Confession, catharsis, or cure? Rethinking the uses of reflexivity as methodological power in qualitative research. *International Journal of Qualitative Studies in Education* 16: 175–196. https://doi.org/10.1080/0951839032000060635.

Secules, Stephen, Cassandra McCall, Joel Alejandro Mejia, Chanel Beebe, Adam S. Masters, Matilde L. Sánchez-Peña, and Martina Svyantek. 2021. Positionality practices and dimensions of impact on equity research: A collaborative inquiry and call to the community. *Journal of Engineering Education* 110: 19–43. https://doi.org/10.1002/jee.20377.

Stein, Sharon. 2020. A colonial history of the higher education present: Rethinking land-grant institutions through processes of accumulation and relations of conquest. *Critical Studies in Education* 61: 212–228.

Open Access This chapter is licensed under the terms of the Creative Commons Attribution 4.0 International License (http://creativecommons.org/licenses/by/4.0/), which permits use, sharing, adaptation, distribution and reproduction in any medium or format, as long as you give appropriate credit to the original author(s) and the source, provide a link to the Creative Commons license and indicate if changes were made.

The images or other third party material in this chapter are included in the chapter's Creative Commons license, unless indicated otherwise in a credit line to the material. If material is not included in the chapter's Creative Commons license and your intended use is not permitted by statutory regulation or exceeds the permitted use, you will need to obtain permission directly from the copyright holder.

CHAPTER 3

Student and Staff Experiences of African Languages in Higher Education

Abstract This chapter examines the responses to questions which were designed to better understand the prevalence of African language teaching in higher education. The chapter explores the experiences of students and instructors in relating to the teaching of African languages in higher education, as well as the other ways in which African languages are represented (or not) across university curricula. It examines the experiences, views and opinions of the respondents as these relate to their experiences of African languages in higher education. Broadly these experiences fall into three categories, positive experiences and reflections, negative or critical experiences, and comments that are linked to more wide-ranging ideas and considerations. Respondents were overwhelmingly positive about the idea of African languages being present in higher education, but have different experiences of the realities of this and the ways in which languages are taught, presented and supported across institutions.

Keywords Students • Instructors • African languages • Representation • Teaching

3.1 Overview

One of the goals of conducting the survey was to better understand staff and student experiences of African languages in higher education. In the institutions we are based at, as well as in the different countries in which

© The Author(s) 2025
H. Gibson et al., *African Linguistics after #RhodesMustFall*,
https://doi.org/10.1007/978-3-031-74817-2_3

we live and work, there is variation between the role and position of African languages and thereby also the staff and student experiences of African languages in their respective higher education contexts.

We are interested in this question for a number of reasons. African languages continue to operate from a position of marginalisation. This is the case both in the African context and outside of Africa, where African languages have been perpetually under-valued and side-lined. As linguists, we are interested in how widespread the teaching and learning of African languages is, given the historical and continued marginalisation.

In addition to better understanding the presence of African languages, we are also interested in which languages were present in higher education and in what contexts. For example, are certain languages more widely taught and learnt than others? Are there differences between this language (or languages) in different contexts? If so, how can this help us better understand the place and roles of African languages and the link between these patterns of decolonisation/transformation?

We are also interested in considerations beyond the presence versus absence of African languages. We are curious about the domains in which these languages are used. If examples from an African language are used in a teaching context, are these embedded in meaningful ways along with information about where the language is used and with who? And are these African language examples presented in such a way that they are exoticised? Are they included as afterthoughts, or otherwise marginalised, or are they part of the core content and focus areas? We are also interested in whether the same (perhaps small group of) languages are used to show a certain feature or phenomenon, in a linguistics class for example. We therefore sought to explore the contexts, the breadth and depth of experiences of African languages and hoped that the responses would help us to better understand these patterns.

In the survey we asked: *"Are African languages taught at your university/institute?"* For the respondents who were students we asked: *"Are you studying or have you studied an African language? If yes, which ones?" "What motivated your decision to study this language/these languages?"* We also asked a broader question which was: *"What courses are offered at your institution that relate specifically to African languages?"* In the current chapter we examine the responses to these questions, as well as responses to an open question that allowed people to share other more general experiences of African languages. In Chap. 4 we specifically examine issues of how perceptible and prominent African languages are in higher education.

3.2 Survey Findings

This section summarises the themes which emerged from the survey responses to our three questions that seek to examine experiences of African languages in higher education. We include some of the example responses, along with information about the participants, where relevant.

We asked *"Are African languages taught at your institution?"* The aim of this question was to help us better understand the spread and prevalence of African language teaching and how many of our respondents were based at institutions where African languages are taught. However, another insight also emerged from the response to this question—a relatively large proportion of the respondents indicated that they did not know whether African languages were taught at their institutions.

The vast majority of participants were based at institutions where African languages are taught. We note that there is likely to be a self-selection bias in our pool of respondents. Since the survey was on African languages and linguistics, there is an increased chance that those who are interested in these issues and/or are based at institutions where these are taught or present completed the questionnaire. However, 119 of our respondents said that African languages were taught at their institutions. This figure can be further broken down to 46 faculty, 23 graduate students, 43 graduate students and 5 'Other'. Some 22 respondents said that they did not know whether African languages were taught at their institutions—9 faculty, 7 graduate and 6 undergraduate. A further 18 responded that African languages were not taught at their institutions, again representing only a small proportion of our overall respondents.

A breakdown of these responses by location provided additional insights. We first examine the teaching of African languages on the basis of respondents based in Africa and those outside Africa; 66 of 77 of the respondents based in Africa said that African languages were taught at their institutions. This contrasts with 53 of 94 of those based outside of Africa who noted that African languages were taught at their institutions. Of those respondents based in Africa, 3 said that African languages were not taught at their institutions, in contrast with 15 respondents based outside of Africa who were at institutions where African languages are not taught. There were 5 respondents in Africa who did not know whether African languages were taught at their institutions and 7 respondents outside Africa who did not know whether African languages were taught at their institutions.

In terms of a breakdown of the responses by role, 70 of 91 students noted that African languages were taught at the institutions they were studying at. This contrasts with 46 of 70 faculty who said that African languages were taught at the institutions where they work. There was a notably higher number of students who did not know (13/91) whether African languages were taught at their institutions. In contrast, 9 of 70 faculty members responded that they did not know whether African languages were taught at their institutions. The difference here between student and staff knowledge and understanding of the broader offerings is perhaps not surprising—faculty could be expected to have a better overall understanding of programmes and options that are available given their likely wider institutional engagement and roles. However, we note that this is likely to have a knock-on impact on student experiences of African languages, views and feelings on prominence and erasure as well as to, in turn, influence views on the link between African languages and social change.

We can also examine the responses from those who said that African languages were taught at their institutions by those who grew up speaking an African language *("Did you grow up using an African language or languages?")* and by those who grew up in environments in which African languages were present (*"Were African languages used in your home or in surrounding areas where you grew up?"*). We consider these questions to be relevant as they provide insights into the presence of African languages in the wider language ecology and how this is (or is not) linked to whether respondents are currently based at institutions where African languages are spoken. For example, this might help us better understand how many respondents who grew up in Africa—or other areas where African languages are present in diaspora communities—are then engaged with and interact with African languages later on in life.

Of those who grew up using an African language at home ($N = 94$), 73 responded that they were based at institutions where African languages were taught (either as students or faculty), 8 marked 'Don't know' and 7 marked 'no'. Of those who did not grow up using an African language at home ($N = 77$), 47 were based at institutions where African languages were taught (either as students or faculty), 15 recorded 'Don't know' responses and 11 marked 'no'. This is therefore a relatively large proportion of people who did not grow up speaking an African language at home who are now based at institutions where African languages are taught. We in part assume that this reflects the overall nature of our respondent pool of people who are at least to some extent interested in or engaged with African languages and therefore completed the survey.

We can also consider the breakdown for the slightly broader question of whether people grew up in areas in which African languages were used in the home or in surrounding areas—here we imagine communities based in Africa who speak other languages, as well as the broader African diaspora communities. Of those who indicated that an African language was used in their home or wider environment (82), 63 responded that they were based at institutions where African languages were taught (either as students or faculty), 8 responded 'No', 6 'Don't know' and we received no response to this question from 8 participants. For those who said that African languages were not used in their home or wider environment (91), 58 responded that they were based at institutions where African languages were taught (either as students or faculty), 13 responded 'No', 16 provided a 'Don't know' response and there were 4 blank responses for this question.

We also asked respondents *"Are you studying an African language?"* 112 of our respondents were studying an African language or languages and 50 were not studying an African language. (17 did not complete this question). We asked respondents *"Are there examples from African languages in your classes?"* For instructors, this relates to the classes they teach while for students this relates to classes they take or are enrolled in; 86 responded 'yes' 7 responded 'no', 6 responded 'don't know' and a larger proportion left this question unanswered (82) which we can perhaps also assume to include a number of people who were not able to answer this question or did not know whether there were examples from African languages in their courses. These responses are discussed in further detail in Chap. 4.

An interesting consideration here in terms of those who responded that they did not know whether African language examples are used in their courses relates to meaningful embedding and change. It is quite possible that an instructor includes numerous examples from African languages (and indeed a wide range of languages more broadly) but that these are simply presented in isolation or as passing examples used to illustrate a particular phenomenon or structure under examination, and without explicit mention of the geographic context. This again highlights the importance of embedding knowledge and ensuring that languages are not presented as unbounded abstract entities that are separated from the communities that use them.

A number of those who did not answer this question provided information in the follow-up question on which African language(s) were taught at their institutions. For those who indicated that African language examples were used in class, we asked "*Which languages and which classes?*" the responses to this question are explored in Chap.4.

3.3 Emergent Themes

In addition to asking about whether African languages are taught at their institutions, at the end of the survey we asked *"Is there anything else about your experience with African languages that you would like to share?"* It is notable that a large proportion of the responses to this question related directly to learning and teaching of African languages. As such, we include here the key themes that emerged from the responses to this question.

Responses to this field were open-ended and we performed an initial round of coding. No prior categories were established or employed and the coding system was determined based on our interpretation of the responses themselves. We divide the responses into three broad thematic categories: (1) positive experiences and/or support for African languages in higher education; (2) negative experiences and broader criticisms; and (3) other ideas, reflections and considerations.

3.3.1 *Positive Experiences and Support for African Languages in Higher Education*

Respondents shared positive experiences of studying African languages, either in the present or the past. A number of the respondents commented that learning an African language had served to open up either their worldviews and perspectives, or had led to specific career paths and opportunities. For example, P244, a White faculty member based in South Africa, noted:

> I have found learning isiXhosa to be one of the most valuable things I've ever done. It's changed the way I relate to the world around me and to my subject matter as a linguist. I only regret not having started sooner.

Similarly, the exposure to learning African languages is credited by one of our respondents, P139, a White faculty member based in North

America, as being the reason they pursued their particular career path and research trajectory:

> I would not be a linguist were it not for the fact that African languages were taught at the universities I attended.

This impact on career path and future directions is also reflected in the response by P84, a White researcher from North America who shares a similar sentiment:

> My exposure to African languages fundamentally changed my life: my career trajectory, my politics, my view of myself.

This respondent links their exposure to African languages not only with a change in career path but also a broadening of worldview and their conceptualisation of the self. It is interesting to see an explicit mention of politics in their response as well, perhaps reflecting the broader (political) positionality of African languages. If African languages continue to operate from a position of marginalisation, then the opportunity to engage with and be exposed to African languages—particularly in a formal context such as higher education—can be quite transformational. The response from P161, a Black African academic not based in a language/linguistics department, also considers the broader impact of using African languages and the impact on the people they are speaking with:

> I love them. They make me feel rooted. Every time I speak these languages I announce myself to whichever audience is hearing. When others learn them as an academic exercise, without Western validation, I feel that respect is being given to African people and civilizations and their contributions to knowledge.

Whilst they do not explicitly mention their politics, in their response appears to be a feeling that the use of an African language—at least in some contexts—is political. The mention of "contributions to knowledge" also speaks to themes related to decolonisation and transformation, which we explore again in Chap. 6. The potential to impact worldview and outlooks is also echoed in the response by P200, a White postgraduate student based in Europe who also talks about the way in which learning African languages has expanded their worldview:

> I think learning African languages has opened me up to so many different perspectives, simply the contact with people, literature, media etc. has expanded my knowledge on pretty much everything in ways I would have never imagined. I think they (and other non-European languages) should be taught at every educational institution.

The link to the broader impact of learning African languages in this context can also be analysed as part of a decolonial praxis. In this response, there is an explicit mention of "non-European languages". While this goes beyond African languages, there is a recognition of the relative power, for example, of European languages in this comment and the different positions of relative power from which different languages operate.

P19, a Black undergraduate student based in South Africa reflects on the role of African languages in terms of improved cultural understanding:

> I think the more we expose ourselves to African Languages the more we can learn and understand people's cultures better.

While the motivations and backgrounds of our respondents differ greatly, several comments highlight the hope that African languages could create an exposure to knowledge about Africa, its peoples and/or cultures that is not currently part of curricula in higher education either inside or outside of Africa. We return to this point below, where we see themes relating to cultural understanding as part of the discussion on the broader context and considerations for learning African languages.

3.3.2 Negative Experiences and Criticisms

In addition to the more positive comments related to experiences of African language teaching and learning, there are also respondents who shared more negative experiences and/or criticisms of their experiences of African languages in higher education. One of the key themes that emerges within the broader reflections relates to the teaching itself, and perhaps by extension teacher training, support and wider provisions.

There is a clear thread that suggests that the quality and style of teaching of African languages is the cause for criticism here, not the fact that these languages are taught. For example, P215, a faculty member who describes themselves as "African" and is based in South Africa notes:

Teaching of African languages is, in my experience, absolutely terrible. Teachers don't understand even the rudiments of grammar or be able to explain things. I think a lot of the problem is with the Direct Method of language learning. I just don't think it is very effective (for me).

Here the criticism is levelled at the style of teaching and also the knowledge base on which the teachers are drawing. A question which arises here is to what extent this criticism is distinct from criticisms which might be made of other subject area teachers and/or teachers of other languages. It may well be the case that due to under-resourcing and limited institutional (and otherwise) support provided for African languages, teachers are less supported. It may also be the case that being considered a "native speaker" of a language is sometimes considered sufficient qualifications for teaching a language, especially but not only outside of Africa. As such, the expectations on teachers of African languages would be high but the training and preparedness may not be equal to these pressures. Such a situation would speak also to the wider marginalisation of African languages and the lack of broader understanding of how the languages function, including but not limited to their grammars. For example, scholars have reported how historical misconceptions of African languages as 'simple' affected their documentation (Deumert and Mabandla 2017). Such an inaccurate—and indeed racist—worldview could add to and perpetuate the misconception that African languages would therefore be easy to learn and easy to teach. It may also mean that people consider the only 'qualification' required to teach an African language is to speak or use it. P202, a postgraduate linguistics student based in Europe, simply states that teaching of African languages in higher education is "underdeveloped". The interpretations and causes of this are no doubt multiple but this statement speaks to the potential for the teaching of African languages to be greater than it currently is, as well as the potential shortcomings and challenges with the current offering.

P11, a Black lecturer based in Malawi comments:

We need to promote discussion of African linguistics using African languages. The common practice is that the common medium (metalanguage) is [a] European language. As a speaker of an African language, I feel I lose a lot in between. Second, linguistics studies written language, the disparity between the spoken and written African language is so big. For example, many studies on relative clauses in Chichewa do not strongly acknowledge that the canonical way of relativising is by prosodic means not morphosyntactic means.

This response contains a number of insights. There is mention of the de facto language policy in which a European language—often English or the language of the former colonial power—is used as the medium of instruction and the language in which the discourse takes place; here referred to as the metalanguage. The idea that material is 'lost' here is important as this speaks to multiple levels and types of 'loss'. While as linguists we do not agree with the comment that linguistics studies written language, there is an important point here about the disconnect between spoken and written language. While this is often the case globally and cross-linguistically, there are aspects of African languages which mean that this might be more pronounced in certain instances. A large percentage of African languages—most of those with no official educational, media or official status—are not commonly used in written form. For many languages, the written or standard form may also differ significantly from the various spoken forms. A large proportion of African languages are also tone languages, yet writing systems vary as to whether this is part of the writing system or not.

There is also variation in terms of transparency in the writing systems in current use. For example, many have colonial or missionary origins, with varying degrees (including very limited) direct involvement and decision making by speakers of these languages. In the case of South Africa, the orthographies date from the colonial era, despite evidence that native speakers actively contested and shaped them throughout the colonial era as shown for isiXhosa in Deumert and Mabandla (2017)—even those for which revisions have subsequently taken place—and the separations between closely related languages or varieties which were politically reinforced during the apartheid era are problematic (Arndt 2023). In many cases these remain contentious and contested (cf. Alexander 1989; Satyo 1992) and which may even partially explain continuing challenges in relation to teaching literacy and reading "performance" of school children in South Africa, although the causes remain numerous and the possible correlations between the specific standardisation and orthographic choices, linguistic properties and learning outcomes require further study (Arndt 2023; de Vos et al. 2014; Diemer et al. 2015; Probert and de Vos 2016).

Another respondent notes a broader consideration of motivations for learning African languages and the impact that this might have on things such as career opportunities and prospects. We know that in language policy terms, English may be favoured by students and parents as a global language of commerce and international mobility which is perceived to increase employment opportunities (Coleman 2011). This is in part reflected in the comment of P28, a Black graduate student based in South Africa who asks:

> Why are we motivated to learn them when still after school they are not taken seriously and working opportunity created afterwards?

However, there is also an acknowledgement in this comment to the broader context in which this teaching takes place, quite separately to career prospects and employment. The comment that African languages are perhaps not taken seriously also reflects a broader experience and expectations related to African languages. This also appears to be the case even amongst populations who think it would be (or would have been) good to have more chances to learn an African language, including for practical purposes. For example, P216, a White linguistics student based in South Africa notes:

> I really wish that I had been taught an African language in primary school like I had been taught Afrikaans as an L2; I feel it would have been more beneficial to me than Afrikaans.

P33, a Black graduate student from West Africa, makes reference to external views relating to the use of African languages and the ongoing devaluation not just of African languages but, by extension, also their speakers.

> [M]aybe the fact that some people including Africans consider me less intelligent and late compared to modernity when they listen to me express myself in African languages. When they tell me in person, I remind them that they are the ones who are behind on a lot of things.

This comment speaks to one of our key concerns and questions that motivated the study. We are interested in exploring to what extent enduring negative perceptions of African languages and the ways in which these impacted the presence, use and views towards these languages continue to shape higher educational contexts. If we take universities and colleges to be sites of higher learning, then an examination of the use of African languages in these contexts can be revealing in terms of how these languages are viewed in relation to scholarship, and the advancement of science and knowledge. Many of these views may not be explicit, but we know that the ways in which different aspects of education and research are supported—or not—impacts learners' experiences and views on what constitutes legitimate fields of study. This may be the result of informal policy, de facto policy and practice. However, formal policies and provisions also have a role to play here. P30, a Black university graduate based in South Africa also reflects on the role of official policy and protections for languages:

> According to the constitution of South Africa we have a language policy that protects and promotes the use of indigenous languages on paper but there is no implementation. And that shows that we are proud of identity but we prefer a foreign language instead of embracing our own African languages. Language Practitioners are experiencing struggles of recognition by the government, working environment and in our society, because our African languages are taken into cognizance.

Official support for African languages, provided by the Constitution of South Africa in this instance, is considered important but also considered to be somewhat tokenistic (see also Chap. 7). The respondent here notes the *de jure* provisions and support but that people still "prefer a foreign language". They also note the challenges language practitioners face in a practical sense when it comes to work and society more broadly, reflecting some of the wider considerations linked to employment opportunities also shared above.

3.3.3 Other Ideas and Considerations

The third broad category of responses we present here relate to other issues, ideas and considerations. For example P123, a White postgraduate student based in the UK and not studying language/linguistics said "[I] don't really have experience with African languages." This was a response we expected to encounter more in our data than we did. Thinking specifically about formal education and the opportunities at higher education, P131, a mixed race (White and South Asian) student based in the UK notes that they have been exposed to African languages but not in the context of formal education:

Any interaction or education i have had of African languages has been entirely independent from academic study

P211, a mixed race lecturer based in South Africa commented on the need for (further) conversations around support for African languages. But they also make a comment about African cultures (and the link between the two):

African languages need to be provided opportunities to develop and [be] appreciated. It is imperative that serious conversations take place around African languages and cultures. There are varieties of African languages which also need to be understood on a larger scale.

This respondent also suggests that further opportunities are needed for African languages to "develop". This appears to be a sentiment which is slightly different from that of P202 above who suggested that the teaching of African languages was 'under-developed'. Here the respondent seems to be suggesting that the languages need further development, perhaps in terms of support and opportunity. But there is also a wider discussion of developing new terminology for evolving contexts and wider domains of use.

While we are interested in the link between African languages and decolonisation and/or transformation, we also note that for many of our respondents these are not linked, or for some they had not thought of the two domains as being potentially linked (see also the discussion in Chap. 6). For example, P87, a White postgraduate student based in Germany, explicitly notes: "I just love learning from the best. I didn't think of it as decolonising". While some of our respondents see the use, support for and promulgation of African languages as intrinsically tied up to the decolonial process, others see these as distinct—or indeed—unrelated aspects.

In terms of other practical comments, P148, a White doctoral student based in North America, reflects on the other ways in which people (and perhaps students in particular) might engage with and encounter an African language, or minoritised languages. This response relates specifically to teaching and training opportunities and perhaps also reflects considerations for how students may become interested in particularly language or language families during the course of their study and/or research:

There should be something between true field work and typical foreign language study. Departments usually make a point to teach major languages, but many linguists would jump on an opportunity to spend serious time [on] even more minor/understudied languages.

P27, an African "language practitioner" based in South Africa makes a comment that speaks to a wider range of contexts in which African languages could—and should—be used.

> Let there be non domination of English in Research, translate research content questions in African Languages eg Setswana and invite responses.

They comment on the use of African languages in the research context. Here they suggest using Setswana as a medium through which to conduct research, moving away from the hegemony of English and other European languages in research.

P16, a Black student based in South Africa, suggests that African languages should have the same space in higher education as other languages:

> African languages are 'languages' just like English, Spanish or French. They are a means of communication. To not have them in higher education is as difficult as it is for non African who don't know a thing or hear a thing in an African language.

This is a sentiment also expressed by P21, a Black undergraduate student based in South Africa, who says:

> They are as important as the western languages and should be given value too.

The response from P26, a Black undergraduate student, also calls for a diversity of African languages to be used in higher education and not to present a single story or narrative through the teaching of a small sample of African languages:

> Just that we should normalise having more than one range of African languages in higher education institutions so that we get to experience the world in different angles. Language has power [to] make and change things.

This is a view that links to some of the issues we explore in further detail in Chap. 4 on ensuring a breadth and depth of African languages are presented in context, in our educational systems. P244, a White faculty member in South Africa, also made reference to differences of experiences and inequalities within their context. They commented:

> I think South Africa would benefit greatly if more English/Afrikaans speakers learned an African language.

This comment can be seen to reflect inequitable patterns of language learning, in this case in South Africa, but perhaps also reflected more widely. While they note that it would be beneficial if more English/Afrikaans speakers learn an African language (a comment which can also be presumed to reflect a racial difference in language learning with "English/Afrikaans" perhaps here serving as a proxy for White) there is also perhaps a nod to differences in language learning here where more speakers of other "African languages" learn English and Afrikaans than the other way around, again reflecting the enduring marginalisation and devaluing of African languages. This is a point which links to issues of erasure and perceptual salience which we explore in further detail in Chap. 4.

P12, a White student based in South Africa, also makes an explicit comment about the importance of language learning and emphasises the role of formal education in this process:

> Children should be exposed to African languages from an early stage in schools and should also be taught the history of cultures to create a better understanding

As can be seen from their comment, not only do they call for African languages to be included from early years schooling, but their comment also suggests a perceived link between language and culture, and thereby improved relations and between groups—and perhaps improved pride in African languages and cultures overall.

Finally, P264, a White student based in Europe provides the following comment:

> A premise that I find worth mentioning is to be aware that one is stuck in one's head: I can only imagine in part what it is like to learn an African/non-European language as an adult/past childhood and vice versa (for the other person); with that in mind, I hope our discourse can be more gracious and open.

This seems to call for a change in perspective and a broadening of thinking, again echoing some of the comments explored in Sect.3.1, a finding on which we will reflect on in Sect. 3.4 below and which will be examined in Chap. 6 below.

3.4 Summary and Reflections

This section combines responses from a range of questions to better understand student and faculty experiences of African languages in higher education. We were interested in the experiences of those within Africa, and outside Africa. Our goal was not to describe the policies in place (which we leave to scholarly research on that topic), but rather, given that the diversity of language-ideological contexts, sociolinguistic ecologies, and material realities across contexts, to learn more about what students and faculty may be bringing into the classroom.

In the survey responses we see evidence of widespread teaching of African languages, and relatively widespread awareness and understanding of the wider presence of African languages at the institutions. However, we also perhaps see some evidence of low salience and/or erasure where some teaching staff report not knowing if African languages are taught at their institutions. We consider this to be part of a broader issue in terms of the perceptual salience of African languages as explored in the next chapter, although since this was not a comparative study we cannot say whether respondents were more/less aware of the teaching of African languages, for example, than European languages. However, since African languages operate from a different position both historically and in the contemporary moment, this may be something to consider more going forward.

In terms of the themes that emerged, we divided these into three broad categories: positive experiences and reflections, negative or critical experiences and then comments which linked to broader ideas and considerations. The positive comments noted how learning and exposure to African languages had shifted respondents' career paths and worldviews, as well as opening up space for exchange with a wider set of people and possibly facilitating exchange and improved cultural understanding.

The more negative comments or experiences primarily related to the teaching of African languages, broader support and the way in which the teaching of these languages is under-developed in some respondents' views. It is therefore not the teaching of African languages which is criticised here, but more the broader context and perhaps style/quality of the way in which some of the languages are taught.

Finally, there were respondents' comments that we have categorised as broader considerations that are wide-ranging. These linked to the different contexts in which respondents are exposed to African languages, with some noting that anything they had learnt was entirely separate from academic contexts. People also commented on the need to introduce learners to African languages from an early age—perhaps particularly relevant for those based in Africa but certainly not exclusively. Respondents also highlighted the need for diversity in opportunities and options to ensure that there was not just a single narrative of an African language presented or that what was available was not tokenistic. A number of the respondents also reflected on the similarities and differences between the positionality of African languages and other languages, particularly highlighting contrasts with European or 'Western' languages.

Respondents also spoke of the need for opportunities and the further development of African languages for wider domains of use, including for example use to conduct research. In the next chapter we explore issues of prominence and erasure of African languages in higher education and return to some of the themes that emerged in the current chapter.

REFERENCES

Alexander, Neville. 1989. *Language policy and National Unity in South Africa/Azania*. Cape Town: Buchu Books.

Arndt, Jochen S. 2023. Zulu vs Xhosa: How colonialism used language to divide South Africa's two biggest ethnic groups. *The Conversation*. May 11. https://theconversation.com/zulu-vs-xhosa-how-colonialism-used-language-to-divide-south-africas-two-biggest-ethnic-groups-204969.

Coleman, Hywel, ed. Dreams and Realities: Developing Countries and the English Language. London: The British Council, 2011. https://www.teachingenglish.org.uk/publications/case-studies-insights-and-research/dreams-andrealities-developing-countries-and.

De Vos, Mark, Kristin van der Merwe, and Caroline van der Mescht. 2014. A research Programme for Reading in African languages to underpin CAPS. *Journal for Language Teaching*. 48 (2): 143–171. https://doi.org/10.4314/jlt.v48i2.7

Deumert, Ana, and Nkululeko Mabandla. 2017. Beyond colonial linguistics: The dialectic of control and resistance in the standardization of isiXhosa. In *Standardizing minority languages*, ed. Pia Lane, James Costa, and Haley de Korne, 200–221. New York: Routledge.

Diemer, Maxine, Kristin van der Merwe, and Mark de Vos. 2015. The development of phonological awareness literacy measures for isiXhosa. *Southern African Linguistics and Applied Language Studies* 33 (3): 325–341.

Probert, Tracy, and Mark de Vos. 2016. Word recognition strategies amongst isiXhosa/English bilingual learners: The interaction of orthography and language of learning and teaching. *Reading & Writing* 7 (1). https://doi.org/10.4102/rw.v7i1.84.

Satyo, Sizwe. 1992. A response to Neville Alexander's essay: 'Language policy and National Unity in South Africa/Azania'. *Southern African Journal of Applied Language Studies* 1 (1): 41–50. https://doi.org/10.1080/10189203.1992.9724591.

Open Access This chapter is licensed under the terms of the Creative Commons Attribution 4.0 International License (http://creativecommons.org/licenses/by/4.0/), which permits use, sharing, adaptation, distribution and reproduction in any medium or format, as long as you give appropriate credit to the original author(s) and the source, provide a link to the Creative Commons license and indicate if changes were made.

The images or other third party material in this chapter are included in the chapter's Creative Commons license, unless indicated otherwise in a credit line to the material. If material is not included in the chapter's Creative Commons license and your intended use is not permitted by statutory regulation or exceeds the permitted use, you will need to obtain permission directly from the copyright holder.

CHAPTER 4

Prominence and Erasure of African Languages in Higher Education

Abstract This chapter examines issues related to how prominent African languages are in higher education, drawing on the broader discourses as well as the views and experiences of our survey respondents. The questions we explore in this chapter relate to the ways in which African languages are—or are not—embedded into different educational spaces and contexts, including beyond language and linguistics classes, for example in history, sociology and economics courses. It also explores whether certain African languages are more widely taught or used to exemplify specific points or topics, and whether there are specific sub-disciplines which make more widespread use of African languages than others.

Keywords Prominence • African languages • Higher Education • Erasure • Absence • Empowerment

4.1 Overview

In Chap. 3 we reflected on the quality and positive or negative experiences of African languages in higher education settings, in this current chapter we zoom in on which languages are visible or not and what this can tell us about our main questions.

We were interested to explore how the study participants perceived the use of African languages in class, either by themselves, in the case of instructors, or by their instructors, in the case of students. We wanted to better understand how salient African languages are and which ones are noticed by our respondents in their various roles as students, instructors or tutors. As our data show, their differing perspectives as students or staff have a major impact on how prominent various African languages are perceived as being.

We asked participants whether any African language examples were used in their classes, to list any such African languages and also the relevant classes. Specifically we asked the questions: "*If there are examples from African languages in the class/es you teach or study, which classes do they appear in? And what languages are the examples from (mention as many as seem relevant)*" in a narrative answer which resulted in a wide range of qualitative data. A total of 78 participants answered this set of questions, with many more answers from faculty members, 49 of 73 participants who identified as faculty members, than from either postgraduate students (16 out of 41 participants who identified as graduate students) or undergraduate students (12 out of 56 participants who identified as undergraduate students).

Again, we note that the self-selection of survey participants led to a large sample of staff who specialise in or teach about African languages and linguistics. While the smaller number of answers from students likely speaks to a lack of prominence of African languages in the classes taken by the student respondents. Of the students who did answer the questions, many were studying African languages or African linguistics, or were based at institutions that focus on African languages/linguistics. A limitation to this exploration is that it only indirectly speaks to the erasure of African languages that we have experienced and noticed in so many contexts and settings.

In interpreting the answers we are interested in seeing which languages appeared, how often they appeared and in which contexts, as well as how this linked to various types of respondents, including students and academic staff, respondents based in different countries, using African languages or not and those in linguistics and those outside of linguistics.

We wanted to explore in which classes African languages appear, in order to gain insights into surface-level, limited context use, such as Swahili alliterative noun classes in introductions to morphology (including infamous examples such as *ki-su ki-refu ki-me-anguka* 'the long knife has fallen'), or 'Khoisan' languages only being mentioned in phonetics due to the presence of click consonants. We also wanted to see if any picture emerged in terms of some sub-disciplines of linguistics that have achieved more inclusion of African languages than others. Based on our own understanding of the linguistic literature and teaching materials, for example phonological theory engages with African languages and African language data to a high degree. For example, data from African languages are often used to better understand—and develop theoretical accounts of—particular tone phenomena such as tone spreading or vowel harmony. This can be seen to contrast with other sub-disciplines of linguistics such as Generative syntax (with the exception of Lexical Functional Grammar), where textbooks rarely reference African languages.[1] However, this pattern did not emerge in our results where the presence of African languages in syntax teaching and classes was mentioned as frequently as for phonetics classes, and more often than for phonology.

We note that, in the broadly divergent global and institutional contexts our survey respondents move in, different ways of inclusion of African languages in different types of linguistics and other types of classes and other higher education settings will be appropriate. However, seeing as African languages account for nearly a third of human languages and their speakers form a significant percentage of the world's population, their erasure from many types of linguistics courses speaks to continued exclusion and bias.

In positive terms, dozens of African languages were mentioned by our participants and many types of linguistics courses were mentioned which reflects a presence of African languages in a number of settings. In fact, one of the participants, P189, a Black academic from West Africa notes:

> Contrary to recent claims, African languages are gaining more visibility in the diaspora. I think African languages are more visible in the diaspora than in the homelands. My study with the Nigerian immigrants in South Africa and other countries supports this.

For another question the same academic notes that making African languages and linguistics visible and including them in the core curriculum is necessary to achieve decolonisation or transformation:

---

[1] We focus on textbooks because of their position in the classroom and in defining fields and scopes of inquiry; however, while the coverage of languages in Generative syntax research continues to be skewed (along the lines of linguistic representations across subfields; Adli and Guy 2022; Collart 2024; Kidd and Garcia 2022) there are numerous syntactic studies focusing on African and other types of minoritized languages.

The link is the visibility of African languages and linguistics in African universities. This entails among others that African languages and linguistics have to be taught in our universities. We need to have more courses in these areas in our [curricula]. We need to make African languages and linguistics study part of the general/basic core courses in our universities. it is only through these processes that we can make them more visible, provide greater level of equity and inclusivity involving African languages, and achieve efficient decolonization/transformation.

This statement in particular rather closely reflects our own thoughts and approaches which inspired this survey insofar as we feel that while many different implementations are needed in different contexts African languages need to be part of a decolonised linguistics curriculum (or, as discussed in Chap. 6, in the creation of a pluriverse linguistics cannon).

While we were also interested to learn how academics outside of linguistics and language programmes perceived or promoted African languages in their classes, none of the participants from other fields answered the question with examples or context discussion.

4.2 Emergent Themes

4.2.1 Salient and Less Salient African Languages in the Survey Responses

Approximately 2000 languages belonging to seven different spoken language families, dozens of signed languages (including local and national ones), as well as a number of Creoles and some isolates are spoken in Africa (Eberhard et al. 2023). These range from being dormant to languages with official status in international organisations and tens to hundreds of millions of speakers. In terms of documentation, for some of these languages only very basic documentation is available, while others are well-resourced and fairly well represented online (such as Swahili). Approximately 80 languages or groups of languages—which means that there is some overlap between these (e.g. isiZulu and Bantu languages or South African Bantu languages)—were mentioned by our respondents.

Close to a third (21) of responses mentioned Swahili specifically as a language which had been featured in linguistics classes. This is unsurprising, seeing as Swahili is possibly the most well-known and widely represented African language in many educational domains, from popular culture to general linguistics textbooks. Another dominant pattern was giving an example of one or more of the nine official South African languages that belong to the Bantu language family (such as isiXhosa, isiZulu or Setswana) which presumably matches the use and promotion of just one of the official languages where the respondent is based. Many South African universities in the provinces where only one of the official Bantu languages is generally used in government and educational settings (which is the majority of provinces for example in the Eastern Cape where isiXhosa is used or the Free State where Sesotho is used) teach only that language and only use that language for official communications. A similar type of response was the clear focus on local languages, irrespective of their official status, such as the response by P40, an academic based in Zambia who listed only languages spoken in Zambia, including Kunda which has under 7000 speakers in Zambia (but many more in neighbouring Zimbabwe):

[...] Cinyanja, [N]senga, Kunda, [T]umbuka, Bemba etc

Likewise, a Nigerian faculty member listed three languages spoken in Nigeria. A faculty member based in Cameroon, P126, named many languages spoken there, as well as more well-known languages from elsewhere in Africa:

Examples from various African languages, some of which are Aghem, Akoose, Bafut, Basaa, Bulu, Duala, Eton, Ewondo, Ghomala, Fe'fe, Ndemli, Medumba, Kom, Mankon, Mboo, Masa, Mafa, Muyang, Giziga, Arab Schwa, Swahili, Kilega, Nweh, Gbaya, Sango, Kanuri, Samba Leko, Zulu among others

Other categorisations which are prominent are genetic with frequent mentions of the phyla or language families partially or exclusively spoken in Africa (such as Niger-Congo, Nilo-Saharan, Afro-Asiatic, 'Khoisan' or subfamilies such as Bantu or Atlantic languages) but also contact languages such as Nigerian Pidgin, and African varieties of former colonial languages including French and English feature prominently here.

Bantu languages accounted for nearly half of the most frequently mentioned languages with Swahili, Chichewa, Bemba and Gikuyu, all of which are large languages which also feature prominently in linguistic descriptions and theory, and all the larger Bantu languages (in terms of numbers of speakers) with official status in South Africa (isiZulu, isiXhosa, Sesotho, Setswana, Northern Sotho (Sepedi)) appeared in this group. Hausa, Yoruba, Arabic, Amharic, Igbo, Somali, Wolof, Akan, Afrikaans, Nigerian Pidgin—all of which are among the African languages with large speaker populations, national or regional status and groups of languages such as Berber, 'Khoisan', Bantu and Cushitic made up the rest.

However, a large number of specific languages were mentioned by the respondents including some that we as authors working on African languages were unfamiliar with. Typically, but not always, these were answers by respondents based in African countries.

Only one respondent named an African signed language, Kenyan Sign Language, in their answer, while another respondent more generally noted data from signed languages as being used in classes. Only a couple of other questions across our survey elicited any answers which mentioned signed languages. Therefore, we might conclude that signed languages are not saliently represented in more general discussions of African languages, a pattern of privileging spoken languages which is also representative of linguistics as a whole (e.g. Hou and Ali 2024). Likewise it appears that linguistics instructors rarely consider signed languages when thinking of African languages. This speaks to intersectional levels of marginalisation within the field.

4.2.2 How Instructors Perceived and Discussed African Languages in the Survey

In this subsection, we analyse specific responses and important themes which emerge from these, starting with perspectives offered by faculty members.

Faculty members, as noted above, provided most of the narrative answers for this question. However, there were detailed answers from participants with different roles, including responses from graduate students in African linguistics, or those based in Departments where African linguistics is taught. This is seen in this answer from P148, a graduate student based in North America:

> In language acquisition, one of the major papers was about the acquisition of passive -w in Southern Bantu. Swahili and Chichewa also appear regularly in syntax and morphology, especially with argument incorporation. In the phonology class, I guest lecture on clicks, in which I discuss Taa, Khoe, and

Kx'a languages, as well as R and S-zone Bantu languages like Yeyi and Xhosa. Dahalo, Hadza, and Sandawe are also mentioned. I am not aware about the rest of the course.

Many participants' answers reflected meaningful engagement with the questions and its wider implications such as reflection of the power and status of various languages. For example P103, a faculty member based in the UK wrote:

> [African language examples] appear in introductory courses on linguistics, typology, morphology, syntax and semantics classes. They are examples from all phyla spoken in Africa. A lot of examples are from languages from the Bantu family, Mande, Atlantic, Berber, Chadic, Cushitic, Nilotic and Khoisan. Usually the languages are big and powerful languages such as Swahili, Hausa, Yoruba, Somali, Chichewa but I also use examples from les[s] powerful and well known (from a European perspective) languages.

The answer by P103 also notably includes languages representing the major phyla and all regions of Africa. This seems to be reflective of the attempt to be as representative as possible of the breadth of African languages in a range of classes. Also noteworthy is the consideration of the unequal status African languages have in respect to each other and in terms of their notability.

Another frequently noted comment by faculty is using languages that they work on themselves as reflected in the statement by P233, a faculty member based in Europe.

> I mostly use examples from my own work in the languages mentioned above, as well as examples from "the literature".

Similarly P187, a faculty member based in the UK, states:

> Apart from the languages I have worked on myself (Hausa, Kenyang, Cameroon Pidgin English), the only constraint is whether there is a grammar available. I have over the years ordered every African language grammar I can find for our university library.

Somewhat different perspectives were offered by academics based in South Africa. In this case by two respondents who do not teach linguistics, such as P32 an isiZulu-speaking South African academic teaching academic literacy to medical students "I greet in all languages; I allow students to interact in their languages and report in English; I allow questions in any language (IsiZulu; IsiXhosa; Afrikaans)" and P80, an isiXhosa-speaking South African faculty member teaching in an African languages programme who wrote "African Literature classes in all nine South African official languages including dialects". What comes out here is the idea that a small set of official/national or regional languages represents 'all' languages, but note that P80 is more precise in their wording. From these answers we do not know if these are all the languages that students have in their linguistic repertoires but this seems somewhat unlikely. In positive terms this reflects some effort at engagement with and accommodation of students' linguistic repertoires. But it is easy to see how this could lead to the erasure of perspectives and needs of the students who use or would prefer to use other languages. These types of statements might also be seen as pushback towards the problematic attitude of treating English, and less so Afrikaans, differently from the Bantu languages with educational and official status in South African higher education and more broadly in South African society.

In South Africa degrees, majors or postgraduate studies in African languages are not as accessible to students as other languages including English, Afrikaans and or even in some instances foreign languages. South African universities rarely offer more than one or two of the nine official Bantu languages as subjects or degrees. Moreover, students cannot study an African language as a so-called home language ('home language' is the South African term for 'first language') if they did not take that language as a high school exit-level course and in contrast to other languages, an undergraduate degree in an African language which has been studied as a non-home language does not allow students to progress to postgraduate study in that language. These factors combine to hinder increasing use of Bantu languages both at university level but also outside of this context. There also tends to be a racialised, unbalanced acquisition of the languages across the country more widely with Black South Africans learning English and perhaps also Afrikaans. In contrast however, very few White or other non-Bantu language speaking South Africans acquire communicative competence in a Bantu language.

Another South African faculty member, P220, who teaches academic literacy shares the view expressed by P32 of appropriate-language use, while also including a broader range of materials from elsewhere in Africa.

i always draw in examples from african languages when teaching about academic literacy and the analyses of different texts in the humanities and social sciences. I've used South African languages, and other examples from e.g. Gikuyu (Ngugi wa Thiong'o [sic]), Nigerian Pidgin, African scripts such as ajami, isibheqe. Also, co-lecturers who speak african languages and afrikaans use them in lectures (a translanguaging approach). Students are also allowed to submit essays in any language, including codeswitching in essays[2]

Two of these answers reflect the overwhelming focus by South African academics on the official languages only and the problematic perception that these are "all languages" that could be relevant to their students. The comment also alludes to the fact that language, identity and race remain strongly linked in South Africa. Despite the fact that many South Africans are multilingual, this is not evenly distributed, as noted above. South Africans who did not grow up speaking a Bantu language, rarely learn any Bantu languages while speakers of Bantu languages nearly always speak some English and/or Afrikaans. Answers from students and staff based in South Africa primarily mention isiZulu and isiXhosa, the two largest languages in South Africa in terms of first language speaker numbers, or the official languages more broadly.

While the interpretation of the question is a bit different from the types of linguistic courses and structures that are found in many of the other answers, the strong focus on local languages is shared with many responses by linguistics faculty and students.

A number of students noted that the prominence of particular African languages was connected to their lecturer's research focus on these languages. For example, P203, an undergraduate student of linguistics and anthropology in North America provided a detailed answer reflecting that a wide range of African languages are visible in several of their classes and how this is influenced by instructor expertise and linguistic repertoire:

> Yes, most of my classes have done fieldwork with African languages. I've had examples in Intro to World Languages, Phonology, and Languages of Africa at least. We've talked about and seen examples from all of the language fami-

---

[2] We have opted not to edit the original text of our respondents. But we note here the ways in which different spellings of people's names (and language names) can add to erasure and reinforce colonialist practices. The name here is more commonly written as Ngũgĩ wa Thiong'o.

lies in Africa. My teachers have worked with Gumuz and Northern Mao, and another professor speaksAmharic so I have also seen a lot from that.

A graduate student based in Germany, P200, also notes a number of linguistics and other types of classes where a range of African languages were core parts of assessments:

> Phonetics, Language classification, Morphology (Burunge, Iraqw), Phonology (Kanuri), Syntax (Hausa, Swahili), Literature (Hausa) --> the languages in brackets were the topics of my finals but there were other African languages used as examples throughout the course

4.2.3 Contexts Where African Languages Appear

In the responses received, participants gave less details of the classes and contexts in which the African languages they mentioned appeared than the languages themselves. Out of the 78 answers, 53 mentioned the classes or contexts. This is likely to be a result of how the question was framed and a different setup might have improved the richness of the data for this aspect. Notably many instructors responded by saying they use examples from African languages in all classes or aim to do so; 10 out of 53, that is about a fifth of the answers—mentioned the contexts in which African languages were present.

This was also noted by students in programmes and departments that focus on African languages. Syntax and phonetics classes were each mentioned 12 times, followed by phonology (11), morphology (8), sociolinguistics (7) and introductory linguistics courses (5) and field methods/language documentation (5).

Another type of answer that appeared several times was that respondents mentioned African languages being used in the classroom by students who were speakers of the languages, rather than forming part of the set curriculum. This may be part of a more carefully planned translanguaging-inspired approach such as noted in the answer given by P25, a faculty member based in South Africa:

> In my Honours class, the students are asked to do a language portrait and reflect on their linguistic repertoire in an essay. They can use any language or variety they want. While the students do not take up the challenge to

write the entire essay in a language aside from English, they do write parts of it in other languages. Examples have been mainly isiXhosa.

Our respondents mention many different types of linguistics classes, from the expected phonetics, phonology, morphology and field methods to experimental linguistics, semantics, language acquisition, and different types of sociolinguistically focussed courses, as well as multiple mentions of syntax.

Some respondents provided very detailed and contextualised answers (see the response from P148 in Sect. 4.2.2).

For example, P114 a graduate student based in the Netherlands provided the following response:

> Information Structure/Syntax – examples of how Bantu word order is conditioned by relations such as focus, e.g. locative inversion constructions; focus marking in different languages, e.g. Aghem; ellipsis in Swahili Descriptive linguistics/phonology –tone analysis of African languages (I taught a class on the tonal system of Luganda)

What we cannot really see from this data is an overall sense of whether the survey participants feel that African languages are sufficiently visible in linguistics modules. There was also no space to address how this should play out in different settings (geographical, institutional) or across different types of courses or at different levels of study. However, participants touched on some of these issues in other answers that we discuss in subsequent chapters.

4.3   SUMMARY AND REFLECTIONS

The responses to our survey reflect that, for some academics and their students, and in some contexts, African languages have gained, or long held considerable prominence. But this often reflects the participants' location in Africa or in a department or programme focused on Africa. Alternatively it may reflect their individual research trajectories or the trajectories of their instructors rather than a general trend in linguistics programmes.

To some extent the answers given by our participants are encouraging in terms of the number and range of languages listed, the number of participants who listed languages of different types and families from across the continent, and the broad range of linguistics of classes they appeared in. Yet, the responses also reflected that the erasure of African languages in higher education remains pervasive. It is not always clear whether the participants overall experienced meaningful and representative engagement with African languages. Certainly some did and provided detailed responses, but other cases this might have just reflected any mention of African languages in a course.

Moreover, at least in settings such as South Africa, the current presence of South African Bantu languages in linguistics curricula is a relatively recent change in many departments, as shown in de Vos and Riedel (2023). As reported there and also reflected in many responses to our survey, the perspective of what is an African language and which languages to include is very much limited by the current list of official languages in South Africa.

In the next chapter we explore the role of African languages in transformation and decolonisation, exploring respondents' engagement with these issues and their perceived link between these wide-ranging issues.

REFERENCES

Adli, Aria, and Gregory R. Guy. 2022. Globalising the study of language variation and change: A manifesto on cross-cultural sociolinguistics. *Language and Linguistics Compass*. 16: 5–6. https://doi.org/10.1111/lnc3.12452.

Collart, Aymeric. 2024. A decade of language processing research: Which place for linguistic diversity? *Glossa Psycholinguistics* 3 (1). https://doi.org/10.5070/G60111432.

De Vos, Mark, and Kristina Riedel. 2023. Decolonising and transforming curricula for teaching linguistics and language in South Africa: Taking stock and charting the way forward. *Transformation in Higher Education* 8. https://doi.org/10.4102/the.v8i0.200.

Eberhard, David M., Gary F. Simons, and Charles D. Fennig, eds. 2023. *Ethnologue: Languages of the world*. 26th ed. Dallas, TX: SIL International.

Hou, Lynn, and Kristian Ali. 2024. Critically examining inclusion and parity for deaf Global South researchers of color in the field of sign language linguistics. In *Inclusion in linguistics*, ed. Anne H. Charity Hudley, Christine Mallinson, and Mary Bucholtz. Oxford: Oxford University Press.

Kidd, Evan, and Rowena Garcia. 2022. How diverse is child language acquisition research? *First Language* 42 (6): 703–735. https://doi.org/10.1177/01427237211066405.

Open Access This chapter is licensed under the terms of the Creative Commons Attribution 4.0 International License (http://creativecommons.org/licenses/by/4.0/), which permits use, sharing, adaptation, distribution and reproduction in any medium or format, as long as you give appropriate credit to the original author(s) and the source, provide a link to the Creative Commons license and indicate if changes were made.

The images or other third party material in this chapter are included in the chapter's Creative Commons license, unless indicated otherwise in a credit line to the material. If material is not included in the chapter's Creative Commons license and your intended use is not permitted by statutory regulation or exceeds the permitted use, you will need to obtain permission directly from the copyright holder.

CHAPTER 5

The Role of African Languages in Transformation and Decolonisation

Abstract This chapter explores how respondents' positionalities (institutional, linguistic, and geographic) shape their perspectives on the role of teaching African languages in decolonisation and transformation efforts. We found that instructors who are more removed from experiences of being colonialised had different perspectives on the role of teaching and learning African languages in decolonisation efforts from those instructors whose classrooms are located in a context where students grew up using African languages. Students had more positive views, and connected increased attention to African languages in the classroom to material benefits for African language users outside of the classroom. The positionality of respondents with respect to African languages, for example whether these languages are ones that they grew up with or languages which they study, was a relevant factor in interpreting the responses to the question of what role there might be for African languages in decolonisation and transformation efforts. Responses suggest that, from a pedagogical perspective, instructors should keep in mind that the potential value of contextualised inclusion of African Languages in linguistic curricula for undergraduate students, particularly in Africa, may be significant for those who grew up using these languages amidst the ongoing marginalisation of these languages.

Keywords African languages • Decolonisation • Transformation • Valence • Risks • Positionality • Solidarity

5.1 Overview

As linguists, the pedagogical scope and tools available to us to address social justice issues such as transformation, decolonisation, or racial justice can feel limited. Including examples from languages and varieties of languages used by communities who have experienced oppression is one approach which linguists have turned to, and the workshops put on by the Semantics and Linguistic Theory (SALT) conference (SALT(ED)), which began in May 2021 and has continued thereafter), as well as the April 2022 Workshop on Linguistic Equity and Justice at University of Toronto are examples of spaces linguists have created to share resources to create problem sets and lessons focused on understudied languages and varieties. These examples come from the North American context, and are largely faculty- or institution-led efforts.

We were curious what participants in our survey, who are a mix of faculty and students, and the majority of whom grew up and were currently located outside of North America, thought the role of African languages might be in the process of decolonisation or transformation. We asked participants *"What role do you think studying and learning about African languages plays in processes of decolonisation, teaching for social justice or transformation of higher education?"*

Responses were open-ended, and the initial round of coding was done using a version of Grounded Theory (cf. Heath and Cowley 2004), whereby the main verbs/predicates in each response were identified and used to summarise the response. Using this method, emergent categories of responses were identified. In a second round of coding, these summaries were made more uniform, so as to identify emergent themes, and, upon examining the resulting labels, a third round of coding categorised each response by its valence (*positive, critical/negative, neutral, mixed*). At each stage, the codes were determined based on the responses themselves, following approaches from qualitative research.

5.2 Emergent Themes

This section summarises the themes which emerged across responses to our question: *"What role do you think studying and learning about African languages plays in processes of decolonisation, teaching for social justice or transformation of higher education?"* Example responses are included, with some information about the participant, including location (broadly categorised in order to preserve anonymity), stage in academia (undergraduate, graduate, or faculty), and self-reported race/ethnicity.

Some participants mentioned that bringing African languages into the classroom serves to increase their perceived value for speakers of these languages, promoting language maintenance and cultural pride. For example, P13, an undergraduate student studying in South Africa from a mixed racial background, wrote:

> No one person will feel either superior or inferior to the next because of the language they speak or the quality of the language they speak. Previously disadvantaged young adults will have an opportunity to flourish in society despite the challenges they may have faced.

P28, a Black graduate student studying in South Africa, said, "It will motivate children to take their African Languages at [a] high level like English and Afrikaans, that they also can be taken as serious." A piece of crucial context here is that English and Afrikaans continue to have hegemony in the context of South Africa and are disproportionately supported, despite official language policies which advocate multilingualism; the student here is highlighting how there is still a need for further support, material and symbolic, for African languages in institutional spaces. P137, an undergraduate student studying in the UK from an African ethnic background said simply: "Learn a language, preserve a culture."

Relatedly, some respondents discussed how legitimisation of African languages can contribute to cultural solidarity and unity across users of African languages, facilitating social change. P15, an undergraduate student studying in South Africa from an African ethnic background, wrote, "It educates and empowers while giving us confidence and pride in who we really are." P5, also an undergraduate student studying in South Africa, from a South Asian ethnic background, wrote "By becoming more consciously aware and educated about the dynamics, power struggles and language hierarchies that exist, learners and educators not only become more understanding and empathetic but it also encourages them to engage and be a part of the change." Along these lines, P216, a White undergraduate studying in South Africa wrote:

> It may enlighten students of the struggles L2/3/4 English or Afrikaans speakers may have in higher education and prompt them to put pressure on their institutions to make African languages have a more prominent place in

tertiary education. After all, the majority of South Africa speak an African language as their L1.

Some responses wrote that inclusion of African languages in the curriculum was essential to the process of decolonisation or transformation. P148, a White graduate student studying in North America, wrote:

> Any effort at decolonization without the presence of more Africans (and other colonized groups) in the space is doomed to failure. Allowing a space for a Xhosa class taught by a Xhosa woman likely entails hiring someone who lived through the worst of Apartheid, and thus can educate students and departments on that aspect too. In practice, and to their advantage, language and culture are inseparable.

This comment aligns with a set of responses focused on the value that African languages can give to linguistics as a field, bringing in new perspectives which decentre European languages and ways of knowing. Notably, this comment also puts an expectation on the imagined isiXhosa instructor, to bring their personal traumas and experiences into the classroom for the purpose of educating (mostly White) students. This type of expectation is not uncommon in North American "diversity" spaces, where instructors and students whose identities are marginalised are often valued in relation to how they can educate and expand the perspectives of students who come from socially dominant groups (e.g. Evans-Winters and Hoff 2011; Anthym and Tuitt 2019; Wright-Mair and Ieva 2022).

Others discussed how studying African languages could be used to promote cultural awareness or understanding, and promote diversity in the classroom. P195, a White faculty member teaching in Europe wrote "Teaching standard-language-community research forms part of a very Western-centric academic model. Linguistics is increasingly showing that many speech communities do not inhabit standard-language cultures. This could play an important part in decolonising the curriculum and teaching for social justice." P81, a White faculty member teaching in North America wrote "On a high level, I think that learning about other systems (language, culture, society) makes you reflect on your own system(s) and not taking things for granted or normal."

P227, a White faculty member teaching in Europe wrote about the relevance of including African languages in the curriculum as a way to push against harmful colonialist myths:

Generally speaking, I think there are many negative assumptions about African languages being 'simpler' than other languages; if people were better educated about the structures of these languages, it would counter this assumption. For linguists, I think that this would encourage fewer people to rely solely on researching European languages and centering those as the norm.

P229, a faculty member of a mixed African racial background teaching in North America wrote simply that including African languages in the classroom was "[i]mportant to diversify views".

The response from P33, a graduate student studying in West Africa, captures many of the above themes, covering cultural solidarity and value, as well as rejection of colonialist ways of thinking:

> [...] Studying African languages also allows us to learn about [their] speakers, their way of thinking, living and acting. And we discover similarities in their different histories which strengthens among us (among Africans) the feeling of belonging to the same community. This reinforces the feeling of fraternity and invites a particular solidarity.
>
> Proud of their common identity, Africans come together to preserve it, to promote their common values, and thereby reject those of the colonist.
>
> Even more, our languages allow us to convey our history, to make intelligible our aspirations, our values, our beliefs, our representations and finally allows us to express our sensitivity to the world with our own words.

Perhaps in dialogue with these perspectives were responses which were more critical or sceptical of the role African languages could play in decolonisation or transformation efforts, with several respondents saying that inclusion of African languages was necessary but not sufficient, that there is a strong risk of tokenisation or harm associated with careless inclusion of these languages without making other substantive changes, and, finally, some saying that there is no role at all for African languages in decolonisation efforts—that these efforts have to come from outside of the classroom. P11, a Black faculty member teaching in East Africa wrote that there is not and cannot be a role for the teaching/learning of African languages in decolonisation efforts "[u]nless we move away from the rampant tokenism". P139, a White faculty member teaching in North America brought in discussion of the value given to African languages by institutions:

The fact that most universities won't put any money into African languages shows how little they value knowledge and experiences from the continent. Most universities won't hire Africanist faculty or allow faculty to teach Africanist classes. In a world of higher education where students are driven by the desire to get high-paying jobs after graduation, Africa is, seemingly, not seen as a place even worthy of exploiting in a colonialist way, much less exploring in a post-colonial way.

P103, a faculty member teaching in Europe of North African ethnicity emphasised the systemic nature of racism and colonialism:

> If done well [...], teaching African languages and about African languages can play a major part in decoloniality and social justice. [...] for me, it is not ignorance or lack of understanding that creates social injustice. It's a system that does it on purpose, is comfortable and benefits from social injustice and racism (since decoloniality is a form of anti-racism). So linguistics and language teaching can only play a role if it decides to play a role.

P215, an African faculty member teaching in South Africa similarly highlighted the necessity to separate inclusion of African languages from anti-racism or even tolerance:

> [...] I don't think there is a link [between studying African languages and decolonisation/transformation]. I've met people who speak African languages and who have a deep respect for African culture etc. who are perfectly hateful people and deep racists. And I've met people who cannot speak (or who have no desire to speak) another language who are wonderful people who fight injustice wherever they see it. An African language is not a magic bullet to build a more tolerant society.
>
> [...] It would be folly to think that merely the ability to speak a language resulted in an openness of mind when languages are vested in culture – and cultures bring with them their own sources of prejudice and injustice.

Other responses were sceptical but saw a potential role for African language users in leading to change, as seen in this response from P21, a Black undergraduate student studying in South Africa:

> It does not help much as African languages are useless in our country because in the work place they are not used. However, change is in the hands of the higher education students to make in workplaces when they

become managers and politicians they can allow people to express themselves in their languages then African languages would gain value in future again.

Several responses along this line noted that the use of African languages in the classroom was necessary but not sufficient in the process of decolonisation/transformation.

P224, White faculty in Europe wrote about the necessity of looking beyond the classroom:

> Learning about African languages can contribute to the process of decolonisation. However, it is not enough. Students also need to learn about the interconnectedness of this world. I think it is also helpful if students visit African countries during their studies to get to know how people live.

P119, a Black graduate student in North America, wrote:

> I don't think learning (about) an African language is necessarily a decolonizing act. However, I do think requiring students learn an African language if they want an African studies degree, and figuring out how to do that in a way that benefits rather than exploits African teachers and students [...] can set one/ an institution on the path towards decolonizing their African studies programs.

Overall, these themes represented a range of perspectives, but notions of *value* (for African language users, the field of linguistics, students outside of the African context), *power* associated with use in the classroom and society, and *material worth* in the form of funding or employment opportunities, were all relevant frames which were evoked.

Notably, the positionality of students, faculty, institutions, and disciplines in relation to the colonial project and African languages is highly relevant here for interpreting these notions. *Value*, for example, may mean something very different for a student in South Africa who grew up using an African language and wants to continue to do so in their workplace and broader society, as opposed to a scholar whose main interest in a particular language or set of languages might be what they reveal about phonotactics or morphosyntax.

5.3 Valence of Responses

After observing the emergent themes of these responses, we were curious about how positive, negative, or neutral the respondents felt about the role of teaching/learning about African languages in the process of decolonisation or transformation—valence (e.g. Moore et al. 2013; cf. Colombetti 2005). As such, in this section, we report on the valence of responses, which is the third and most abstracted level of the qualitative coding. Based on the first round of qualitative coding, which focused on main verbs and predicates, we identified whether the response indicated *positive*, *negative/critical*, *neutral*, or *mixed* attitudes towards the role of African language teaching in decolonisation/transformation efforts. Some respondents also said outright that they did not know what the role was or if there was a role for African language teaching in such efforts, which was coded as "IDK" for "I don't know."

Table 5.1 shows the distribution of response valence across all participants.

As an example of a *Positive* response, P55, an undergraduate student studying in Europe of mixed racial background wrote:

> [...] If the acquisition of European languages by Africans was a central part of colonisation, I think the reclaiming of African languages by Africans in public spaces, and the acquisition of African languages by non-Africans, can play a central part in decolonisation.

P36, a White faculty member in Europe wrote that the role of African languages in decolonisation efforts is "Very important, it gives value to

Table 5.1 Valence of participants' responses to: "What role do you think studying and learning about African languages plays in processes of decolonisation, teaching for social justice or transformation of higher education?"

	Valence of responses across all participants
Critical/Negative	14
IDK	2
Mixed	3
Neutral	5
Positive	46
Total	70

grounded embodied experiences in specific social and local contexts, as opposed to hegemonic northern and western discourses".

Neutral responses mentioned that including African languages would give more data or increased awareness of African languages, while *Mixed* responses included the positives along with emphasising the risks of inclusion without proper context. For example, P114, a White graduate student in Europe, wrote "If you study the languages you have a much better understanding of them than just looking at the linguistic profile, and you are also exposed to some cultural knowledge. There are risks though of exoticising African languages, and thinking you know more than you do."

The *Negative* and *Critical* responses were initially separated. The *Negative* category represented simple negative reactions to the role of teaching African languages in decolonisation efforts; P41, a White undergraduate studying in Europe simply wrote "not that much" in response to our question. However, the *Critical* category represented responses which were more detailed in questioning the role that African languages could or do play in decolonisation efforts; as these two labels could potentially represent similar approaches and ended up differing mostly in how much detail was provided, we decided to combine them, as they both represented a broadly negative valence.

5.3.1 *Valence of Responses by Role in Academia*

Of course, the natural follow-up to this is to ask who *were* these respondents, and how their own experiences might have shaped their perspectives on the role of African languages in decolonisation/transformation efforts. Shaped by the context of the social movements described in Chapter 1 and keeping in mind our own experiences of how an instructor's intent is not always clear in practice, along with our own scepticism of how much simple inclusion can lead to transformative changes, our team was initially interested in differences between students and faculty in terms of their perceptions about the role of African Languages in decolonisation/transformation processes. As such, we sorted responses by stage in academia (*undergraduate, graduate, faculty, other*). The results are plotted as stacked bar plots in Fig. 5.1, and the numbers for each group can be found at the top of each bar.

In Fig. 5.1, bars represent role, segments represent proportion of responses labelled as the identified valence category, and the number of respondents represented in each bar is listed at the top. Figure 5.1 shows

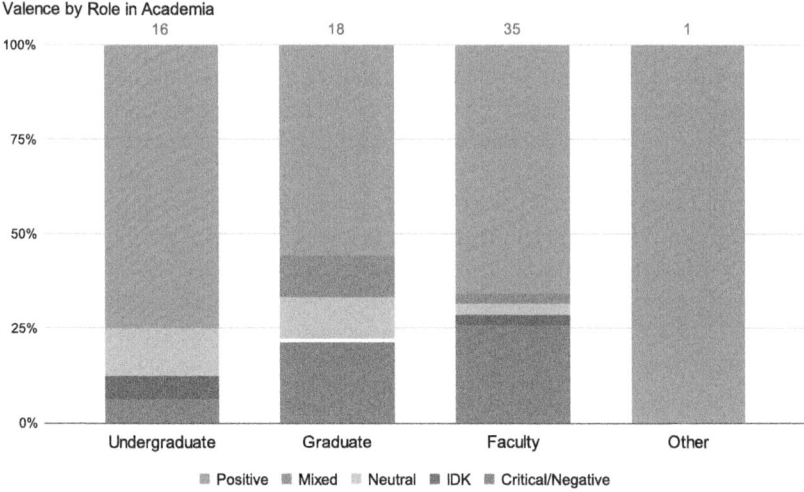

Fig. 5.1 Stacked bar plots representing the valence of participants' responses to: "What role do you think studying and learning about African languages plays in processes of decolonisation, teaching for social justice or transformation?"

a general pattern whereby critical/negative responses increased as a proportion of total responses from undergraduates to graduate students to faculty. Unambiguously positive responses represented the highest proportion of undergraduates' responses, and mixed and neutral responses represented a higher relative proportion in graduate students' responses as compared to the other two groups.

5.3.2 Valence of Responses by Relation to Africa and African Languages

Another potentially relevant way of analysing these responses emerged from our reading of the responses to this question; the role of African languages in the lives of the survey respondents themselves seemed to be important to interpret the responses. As outlined in more detail in Sect. 4.1, some responses stated that studying African languages can increase the status of African languages and therefore be valuable for users of those languages. Other responses focused on the value of African languages in providing different perspectives in the classroom, and still others focused on the value of African languages to the field of linguistics.

Clearly, the positionality of the respondent with respect to African languages, whether these languages are ones that they grew up with or languages which they study as outsiders to the community, can and should influence our interpretation of these responses. As such, we were curious how two of the demographic questions we asked might influence responses to this question. First, we asked if participants who grew up using an African language systematically differed in their responses, and second, we asked if participants who were based in Africa systematically differed in their response from those not based there. Of course, there were several participants who grew up speaking an African language who were not based in Africa, and others who were based in Africa but did not grow up using an African language, so the patterns below should be interpreted accordingly.

Figure 5.2 shows valence of response by participants' current location with respect to Africa specifically, splitting up respondents into two groups. Participants who indicated that they split time between locations and

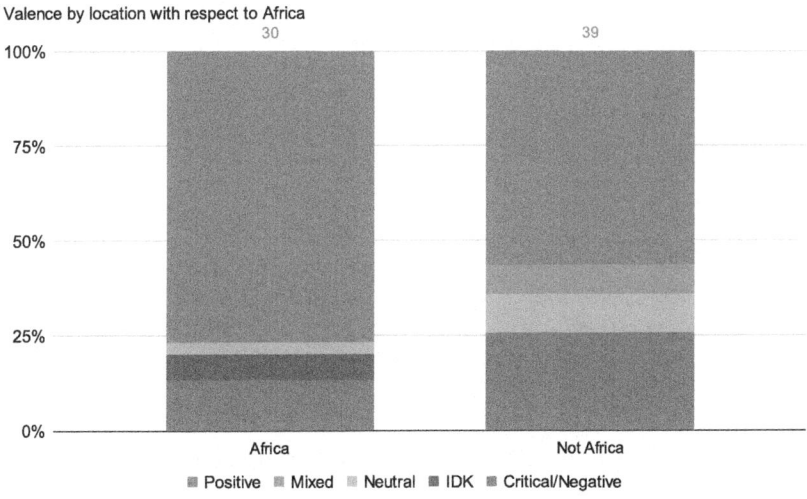

Fig. 5.2 Stacked bar plot of valence of response by whether or not participants currently live in Africa

included Africa as one of those locations were included in the "Africa" category.

In Fig. 5.2, bars represent location, segments represent proportion of responses labelled as the identified valence category, and the number of respondents represented in each bar is listed at the top.

As shown in Fig. 5.2, participants in Africa were more likely to have positive responses as compared to participants not in Africa. This is likely explained at least partially by the fact that undergraduate students were disproportionately likely to be located in Africa, and as shown in Sect. 5.3.1, they also were more likely to give a positively valenced response overall.

Figure 5.3 shows the valence of responses with location broken down a bit more, into very broad global regions. In this figure, we combined the responses from the participants who split their time across regions together into one group ("Europe/North America/Africa").

In Fig. 5.3, bars represent location, segments represent proportion of responses labelled as the identified valence category, and the number of

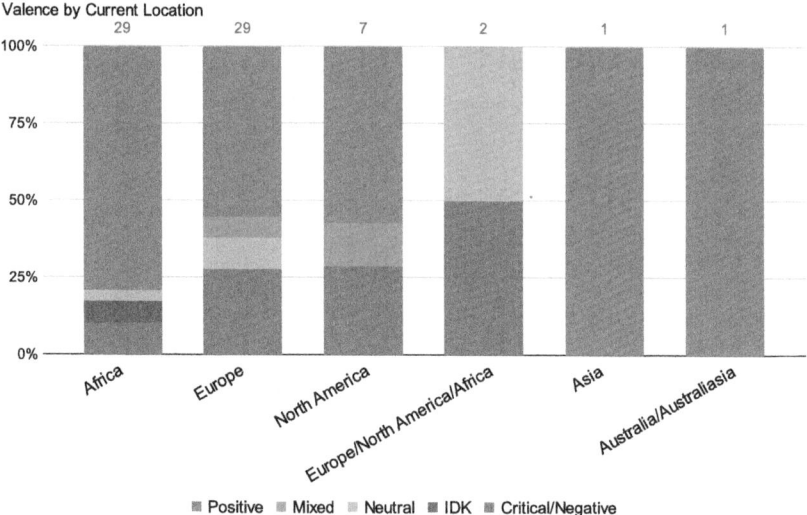

Fig. 5.3 Stacked bar plot of valence of response by current location, broken down into broad global regions

respondents represented in each bar is listed at the top. Here again we see that the critical/negative responses from outside of Africa are coming primarily from respondents located in Europe and North America, and the proportion of faculty respondents in those areas, who were overall more likely to be critical, is much higher. Broad location does not necessarily tell us about participants' personal relationships to African languages; as such, we also asked about valence of response by whether participants grew up speaking an African language. These results are plotted as a stacked bar plot in Fig. 5.4.

In Fig. 5.4, segments represent the proportion of responses labelled as the identified valence category, and the number of respondents represented in each bar is listed at the top.

Of course, all of the nuances and challenges with labelling a language as being "African" which were described in Chap. 2 apply here, as the grouping was done as described therein. In short, we went with participants' own characterisations of their language as being African or not. Here, we do not see a very strong pattern, unlike the role of location. The proportion of critical/negative responses was slightly higher amongst those who did not grow up speaking an African language (22% vs 15%), and the

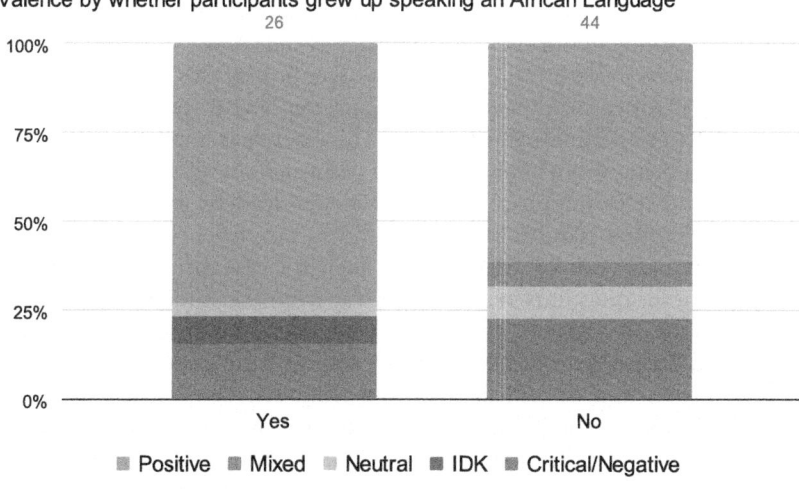

Fig. 5.4 Stacked bar plot of valence of response by whether participants grew up speaking an African Language

proportion of positive responses was slightly higher amongst those who did (73% vs 61%). With this question, there might just be more heterogeneity amongst participants which this coding system did not capture, and we would need to collect some more data in order to make a clear quantitative claim. Regardless, both location and growing up speaking an African language are relevant factors in predicting valence, though different methods would be required to evaluate this claim quantitatively.

5.4 Summary and Reflections

A central theme which emerged from this chapter relates to who decolonisation efforts are constructed as being for. We cannot make sweeping claims like "learning about African languages in the classroom is not part of colonisation efforts" without taking into account the context of students, instructors and institutions. It should not be surprising, and perhaps it is somewhat trivial, that those instructors who are themselves somewhat personally removed from the experience of being colonised should have a different perspective on the role of teaching/learning African languages in decolonisation efforts. Similarly, if one's classroom is located in a context where students grew up using African languages, that should also influence what it means for these languages to be included as part of the curriculum, as compared to classroom contexts in which students are learning about African languages as outsiders.

Faculty were overall more critical and sceptical of the extent to which inclusion of African languages in curricula can lead to transformation as compared to undergraduate students. This likely has a range of explanations, from being more likely to engage with such questions in their disciplinary context to increased time in academia leading to more personal experiences of how harmful tokenised and surface-level engagement with African languages can be. It also is very likely the case that faculty engaged with the survey questions in a different way from the students—providing critique is an oft-engaged muscle for academics, and that impulse likely influenced verbosity in terms of length and content. Indeed, the greater relative proportion of critical responses from scholars outside of Africa perhaps shows a needed reflexivity or awareness of how the positionalities of instructors and students themselves should limit how uniformly positive one can be about the extent to which inclusion can contribute to transformation or lasting, meaningful change (e.g. Ray et al. 2017).

This does not mean that we should see the relative positivity of undergraduate students as being naive or surface-level; many of the "positive" comments engaged with material advantages of increasing the status of African languages, alongside more intangible benefits. Indeed, as scholars working in decolonial theories have argued, the role of those in North America and in the UK in decolonisation efforts has been constructed as more abstract, which we see in the responses from these locations as compared to the more material concerns of students and faculty located in Africa. Further, optimism and positivity, alongside necessary pessimism and critique, have very critical roles to play in transformation and struggles for social justice (Mbembe et al. 2006).

From a pedagogical perspective, instructors should keep in mind that the potential value of contextualised inclusion of African Languages in linguistic curricula, particularly in the African context, may be higher for undergraduates than it may feel for instructors. Outside of Africa, the potential material benefits to language users seem to be understated as compared to the benefits for linguists or linguistics. Overall, making transparent the potential connections between including African languages in linguistic curricula and decolonisation/transformation could go a long way to understanding points of (dis)connection between students and instructors. Racist assumptions which have done and still do underlie the study of African languages need to be rooted out and addressed in instructional contexts, and the necessity and impact of such actions in the classroom will vary according to context. As will be seen in Chap. 6, tokenistic inclusion is harmful, but instructors need not let our critical impulses obscure the potential and perceived value for students.

The next chapter goes on to explore respondents' views and conceptualisations of decolonisation and transformation, with a view to better understanding how these were perceived amongst our respondents.

References

Anthym, Myntha, and Franklin Tuitt. 2019. When the levees break: The cost of vicarious trauma, microaggressions and emotional labor for black administrators and faculty engaging in race work at traditionally white institutions. *International Journal of Qualitative Studies in Education* 32: 1072–1093. https://doi.org/10.1080/09518398.2019.1645907.

Colombetti, Giovanna. 2005. Appraising valence. *Journal of Consciousness Studies* 12: 103–126.

Evans-Winters, Venus E., and Pamela Twyman Hoff. 2011. The aesthetics of white racism in pre-service teacher education: A critical race theory perspective. *Race, Ethnicity and Education* 14: 461–479. https://doi.org/10.1080/13613324.2010.548376.

Heath, Helen, and Sarah Cowley. 2004. Developing a grounded theory approach: A comparison of Glaser and Strauss. *International Journal of Nursing Studies* 41: 141–150. https://doi.org/10.1016/S0020-7489(03)00113-5.

Mbembe, Achille, Olivier Mongin, Nathalie Lempereur, Jean-Louis Schlegel, and John Fletcher. 2006. What is postcolonial thinking? *Esprit*: 117–133.

Moore, Julia E., Brian K. Bumbarger, and Brittany Rhoades Cooper. 2013. Examining adaptations of evidence-based programs in natural contexts. *The Journal of Primary Prevention* 34: 147–161. https://doi.org/10.1007/s10935-013-0303-6.

Ray, Victor E., David Luke, Antonia Randolph, and Megan Underhill. 2017. Critical race theory, afro-pessimism, and racial Progress narratives. *Sociology of Race and Ethnicity* 3 (2): 147–158. https://doi.org/10.1177/2332649217692557.

Wright-Mair, Raquel, and Kara Ieva. 2022. Are we in this alone? Examining the cost of Health & Wellness by surviving the neoliberal academy for multiple Minoritized faculty. *Journal of Trauma Studies in Education* 1: 1–29. https://doi.org/10.32674/jtse.v1i1.3648.

Open Access This chapter is licensed under the terms of the Creative Commons Attribution 4.0 International License (http://creativecommons.org/licenses/by/4.0/), which permits use, sharing, adaptation, distribution and reproduction in any medium or format, as long as you give appropriate credit to the original author(s) and the source, provide a link to the Creative Commons license and indicate if changes were made.

The images or other third party material in this chapter are included in the chapter's Creative Commons license, unless indicated otherwise in a credit line to the material. If material is not included in the chapter's Creative Commons license and your intended use is not permitted by statutory regulation or exceeds the permitted use, you will need to obtain permission directly from the copyright holder.

CHAPTER 6

Views on Decoloniality and Transformation Discourses in African Linguistics

Abstract This chapter examines respondents' attitudes towards the concepts of decolonisation and transformation. Respondents report different views, opinions, experiences and degrees of exposure to the notions of decoloniality and transformation. The chapter explores the ways in which the survey respondents engage with these notions and the key patterns that emerge from this portion of the data. Respondents in South Africa appear to be more closely embedded within discourses on transformation, while outside of South Africa decolonisation is the dominant of these discourses. However, decolonisation also has differing interpretations and appears difficult to narrow down. This suggests the need for a reconsideration and reshaping of our understanding of the role of colonialism, empire and racism in the contemporary world. The chapter shows that making transparent the potential connections between including African languages in linguistic curricula and decolonisation/transformation could go a long way to understanding points of (dis)connection between students and instructors. Respondents also warned against tokenistic inclusion. However, our findings show that instructors should not let their critical impulses obscure the potential and perceived value of supporting the presence of African languages in educational spaces. A strong imperative of doing and not only talking decolonisation emerged.

Keywords Decoloniality • Transformation • African linguistics • African languages • Discourses • Resistance

© The Author(s) 2025
H. Gibson et al., *African Linguistics after #RhodesMustFall*,
https://doi.org/10.1007/978-3-031-74817-2_6

6.1 Overview

Decolonisation, decoloniality and transformation discourses have gained currency in higher education albeit that the first two terms are more pervasive globally. This chapter engages with responses to the following survey question: *"What do the notions of transformation and decoloniality mean to you?"*

Additional background information that formed part of the question stated as follows:

> Different academic contexts and countries use different terms for this. However, the visibility and place of African languages and linguistics is often seen as part of a broader need to decolonise or in some countries the need to transform higher education or more generally achieve a higher sense of equity and inclusivity.

With this question and background, we wanted to explore how the terms decoloniality and transformation are understood among linguistics scholars, particularly related to African Linguistics and its presence in a canon. We also wanted to see how these terms are tied to a transforming or changing higher education sector across the globe (see Sects. 1.2 and 1.3) for a discussion on transformation. It was also important to see the embeddedness of African linguistics in a decolonial and/or transformative project.

To contextualise the participants' responses we briefly reflect on our own views of decolonisation and transformation here. The terms 'decoloniality' and '*transformation*' are often connected but not used synonymously in the South African context. When they are linked, it is to show that transformation could be inclusive of a decolonial project. We recognise that there is no singular understanding of decolonisation or decoloniality but follow Mbembe in viewing these understandings as coalescing in a central question about what knowledge is valued (Mbembe 2019).

Our understanding of (de)coloniality and knowledge production in higher education is shaped by scholarship engaging with the following ideas. The quest to decolonise involves bringing indigenous knowledges, always present but not always visible, into the foreground and a delinking from colonial matrices of power (Mignolo and Walsh 2018). In a colonial academy, theory is produced in the West and applied in other parts of the world (Mamdani 2019) and so we are charged to find new ways.

Decolonisation led to the dismantling of colonial administrations but not to post-coloniality (Ndlovu-Gatsheni 2013) and a world of new knowledges, that works contrary to practices that seek to "take us further and further from ourselves to other selves" (Ngũgĩ wa Thiong'o 1986: 12).

In the midst of decolonisation discourse debates and spaces to 'judge Euro-America deceit' (Ndlovu-Gatsheni 2013), there are ongoing practices that reimagine the received canon, for example Muthien and Bam's (2021) work on reinterpreting indigenous women's pasts as way of recentering African women's historical and sociological knowledge or Makalela's (2016) notions of ubuntu translanguaging that are finding traction in South African institutions. A decolonial process is needed to deepen the impact of decolonisation and decentre Global North knowledge domains. Transformation, on the other hand, is understood to be a catchword for growth and reform in education (Dilraj 2021), meaning that it is broad. It can reference structural and cultural reform and this can include curriculum reform.

As will be seen in the ensuing discussion, participants had different views, experiences and levels of engagement with both of these terms and the broader associated issues. It is valuable for us to unpack these notions among linguistics scholars and students, and to see how they relate to the inclusion (or exclusion) of African languages in a reimagined set of linguistics canons.

6.2 Emergent Themes

Survey participants engaged more with their understandings of the concept of decoloniality than transformation. This could be as a result of a decolonial turn globally (Mignolo 2011) as the concept is experiencing a resurgence globally with a myriad of discussions framed around its nature and enactments. The notion of *transformation*, when considered by participants, was framed as a broad understanding of change. Transformation was seen by some participants as being more value-free or neutral than decolonisation. Most participants expressed positive attitudes towards decolonisation and/or transformation which of course is likely affected by people who hold such views being more likely to have completed our survey. A few participants indicated that they were unaware of both notions. Some also did not see links between transformation and decolonisation.

Looking at the open-ended answers to the question of what transformation and decolonisation means to participants, ten key themes emerged:

disruption and excavation of knowledge; situatedness of transformation and decoloniality; transformation of decoloniality as undoing and (re)doing; decoloniality as erasure; decoloniality as invisible notion; a new metalanguage for the study of African linguistics; decentering the individual as a colonial subject; decoloniality and positionality; decoloniality as self-serving; decoloniality and entrenched Global North power; and decolonial resistance. These themes are discussed here in turn.

Theme 6.1: Disruption and Excavation of Knowledge
Understandings of transformation and decoloniality firstly focused on disruption of normalising Global North-linked knowledge and the excavation of indigenous knowledges that have been invisibilised (Ngũgĩ wa Thiong'o 1986; Mignolo 2011) in the academy. P3, a White faculty member in the UK, saw decoloniality as involving "The way you approach your content and practice, looking at it through a lens of western norms – asking why it is that way, could it be different. Looking at English grammar and looking for its origins in African languages." In this response, attention was given to a deeper exploration of curriculum and pedagogy, that is, what was being taught, where this knowledge came from and how it was being taught and why. This participant's comment also subverts the way African languages are often seen and portrayed, as receiving from rather than shaping dominant global languages. The nature of the knowledge also came under scrutiny and if it constituted liberatory epistemologies. The quest for different ways of knowing and doing was illustrated in the example of English grammar and its links to African languages. This spoke to the desire for conversations about the links between languages.

P259, a Black postgraduate student currently based in Scotland, wrote that "In Linguistics, this would include the study of minority languages … and regarding them at the same level as one does English. It is venturing out with intention to study these other languages and form research questions around them that can be used to build up knowledge and effect change in education, policy making in those countries." Besides adding to a global canon, the excavation of indigenous knowledge is seen here as having the potential to change policy and maybe even society more broadly.

P229, an Afrolatinx faculty member in Canada, zooms in on the nature of the knowledge that needs disruption in "leaving white male western ethnocentric view aside; including more diverse theories, methods, examples, authors".

Theme 6.2: Situatedness of Transformation and Decoloniality
In a number of responses, transformation and decoloniality were understood in their situatedness. Transformation was viewed as a process which could lead towards decoloniality. These notions were seen as subjects embedded within human connections and as inseparable, with decoloniality being seen as an outcome of transformation.

Transformation and decoloniality were seen to have traits of both the global and local as can be seen in the response of P4, a White Assistant Professor based in Germany, "Deep transformation towards a decoloniality reality is a global yet particularised issue." Furthermore, academic discourse should be drawing on "a more connected view of the world, such as African 'ubuntu'", according to P123, a White student in the UK. This UK student shows knowledge of the African concept for relational living but the exact context of her knowing is not clear. From the response we cannot tell if her knowledge is as a result of her formal education or some other exposure. Ubuntu has been described as an African moral ethic (Metz 2011) that speaks to our intertwinements and solidarities with others and that informs our personhood. The implication is that transformation and decoloniality with an ubuntu lens would strengthen human connections globally through their processes.

P215, a Black faculty member based in South Africa, responded that "Transformation is a useful concept involving changing societal structures (education included) to become more inclusive and representative of the people (and their experiences) of the republic (not just in terms of race but also of gender, class etc.)." The implication is that transformation can align to a decolonial curriculum structure that reflects people's experiences.

Transformation and Decoloniality were also used synonymously by participants. For example P226, a White student from the UK uses "Transformation/Decoloniality" in her response. For P81, a White faculty member from Germany "... decoloniality or transformation is an absolute necessity, where I, unfortunately, do not see enough progress being made". They are particularly linked by P81 to "changes for equity and inclusion, for instance in terms of pay rates or equal representation of 'black, female & other minorities' amongst faculty at Western institutions as well as questions of power structures in knowledge transfer are long overdue".

Theme 6.3: Transformation and Decoloniality as Undoing and (Re)doing
Transformation and decoloniality were conceptualised as processes of undoing and (re)doing by the vast majority of participants. The vestiges of colonialism have to be undone, and knowledge has to be recharacterised. This entails a redoing of what such knowledge constitutes, and an active undoing—essentially a dismantling—of this knowledge in practice and theory. Firstly, transformation was seen as a wide-ranging change to societal structures. P5, an Indian student and research assistant based in South Africa, states that "Transformation brings about change, changing the discourses, ideologies and practices of a society or entity" and that "Decolonisation is a process of transformation." P 16, a Black student from South Africa, views decolonisation as "what should be". Comments that "Decolonisation is a process of transformation" (P5) and "These two concepts should be linked, as transforming the institution will also involve transforming what and how we teach" (P244, a White faculty member based in South Africa), illustrate that to these respondents decoloniality is seen as part of the process of transformation of what we do.

The elements of this process are unpacked in P5's response that "It's about engaging in the matrixes, hierarchies and power inequality brought about by/during colonisation." Processes of undoing Global North hegemony of knowledge were dominant in responses about understandings of decoloniality. Decoloniality was described variously, by P5, as "a critique of Eurocentrism and western culture", by P3, a White faculty member based in the UK, as "Undoing your teaching content and practice, looking through a lens of equality rather than an add-on" by P137, a Black student from the UK, as "engaging with resources that do not fulfil this colonial sentiment".

P227, a White faculty member in the UK, links the undoing of knowledge to economic processes "removing a capitalist model of education, where knowledge is commodified and courses are seen as corporate outputs". Corporatisation critiques of higher education have gained traction with arguments that bringing business and managerial practices into higher education poses existential threats to academic and intellectual freedoms, with a neoliberal agenda being favoured (Habib 2013). This survey response links corporatisation to moves away from desired transformative and decolonial processes.

(Re)doing involved "anti-racist work and restructuring academic pursuits to distance them from their colonial histories" (P7, a bi-racial postgraduate student in North America), "decentering" (P214, a White South

African researcher) and the promotion of "equal learning and inclusion" (P5). One respondent was emphatic that undoing and (re)doing was "needed" (P20, a White faculty member in South Africa) while another urged that "Decolonisation is doing. It has been theorised to death" P25 (a Black faculty member and PhD candidate in South Africa). The responses reflect that there has been much soul-searching about what decolonisation and decoloniality is and what it is not. #RhodesMustFall resulted in a fresh slew of literature that mostly theorised the concepts but decolonial teaching practices were also highlighted. The responses discussed here remind us that the doing of decoloniality is what needs to happen for the project to succeed.

Redoing takes on affective and liberatory aspects in "Freedom from … being forced to live in spaces that make you feel trapped" (P15, a Black student from South Africa). This could reference both the material and emotional effects that decolonisation and decoloniality can have on individuals and how they then work "to counteract what are primarily eurocentric or 'Western' approaches to knowledge/ knowledge generation" (P34, a White academic in Ireland). With redoing comes "the dissolution of power structures that either came about under or were used" and "widening participation in HE [higher education]" (P37 a White academic based in the UK). The latter can be said to reference both transformation and decoloniality.

Physical access to higher education is an important aspect of transformation. In many colonised countries this meant giving access to previously colonised subjects which in the South African context happened much more recently, after the end of apartheid, unlike in the countries that became independent in the 1960s and earlier. However, P84, a White postdoctoral researcher in the Netherlands, interrogates the knowledge that is given access to, with "questioning (of) (often subtle) violences that persist and a re-forming of the dominant narratives". The violences of colonialism have become more subtle and are realised in the enduring nature of Global North knowledge and its continual re-emergence.

Colonial powers were referenced directly by P55, a mixed White and Asian student from the UK, with "In Britain, it is about seeing our history warts and all, and addressing the legacies of empire directly. I think the study and use of African languages, including in higher education, can play a central part in this." So P226, a White student in the UK, calls us "To address historic oppression and listen to the horrors the British empire committed." These points were not expanded on but it seems that the impact of colonisation needs to be understood more fully in truth-telling situations. P55's response highlights that African languages are peripheral in higher education in Britain. A way of addressing this and the colonial legacies of Britain in Africa and elsewhere would be to bring African languages to the centre with other global languages. The undoing and (re)doing should not be tokenistic, "as a favour done to indigenous people but should be seen as 'basic education'" (P103, a North African academic based in the UK). This implies that decolonisation endeavours should and must have legitimacy, though without the "need for western validation" (P161, Black faculty member from Ghana) and thinking that "the only 'good' things to study are by White people" (P226, a White student in the UK).

In our survey, decoloniality was linked specifically to the topic of African linguistics, even though the question which we are reflecting on in this chapter was not specifically about African linguistics. For P181, a White faculty member from Scandinavia, (re)doing means "to get the knowledge of and on African languages and their cultural context out of their specialist niche and make them relevant as part of human knowledge". This seems to highlight the fact that African language studies are on the periphery and are not fully legitimised in global higher education spaces. The response could also mean that African languages need to be taken away from being studied as formal linguistic material, and should be studied as sources of knowledge and to see how they reveal different cosmologies.

For P124, a White faculty member in North America, (re)doing involves an openness to "new and different ways of approaching linguistic data, and critiquing what linguistic data even is, anyway, or linguistics for that matter". The canon and its normative methodological frameworks are the focus here. Indigenous methodologies are seen to be under-represented in linguistics and for P195, a White faculty member in the UK, this results in "Our theoretical and empirical bases not sufficiently informed by scholars/scholarly research of the Global South". Care should be taken with "de-exoticising languages" and "the metalanguage used to describe/discuss such languages" (P106, a White academic in the UK). (Re)doing involves assuming a pluriversal account of the world which involves "switching the perspective from Western/Eurocentric lenses to more pluralistic ways of analysing the world. For a start, who teaches what? who writes about what?" (P206, a White student from France) and "bringing in knowledge that is local to allow us to understand our own contexts better and also to reflect on the supposed universality of 'Western' paradigms" (P244, a White faculty member in South Africa). P206's response also raises questions of who has the power to name and from whose worldviews a metalanguage gets developed. In a pluriversal account, the universality of Western knowledge as superior and a closure of other knowledge forms would be erased with the world then conceived of as a pluriverse with different cosmologies and pluriverses of meaning (Mignolo 2011). Scholars are positioned as subjects of their disciplines and fields "to balance agency and ownership and shift it to the global south" (P36, a White faculty member in the UK) to realise a pluriversal linguistics canon.

P25, a Black faculty member and PhD candidate in South Africa states:

> While decolonisation has been theorised to death, and the role of languages has not, in my opinion, been really dealt with aside from scholars like Gabriella Veronelli and Finex Ndhlovu, I agree with Allison Phipps that decolonisation is 'doing'. We have debated the role of African languages for decades. There have been many scholars who have proven that African languages can be used successfully in the classroom. So now we just have to do it.

Though there should be an undoing and (re)doing, it does not involve discarding Global North epistemologies and languages as "I don't think 'colonial' subject matter should necessarily be thrown out, but it should be thoroughly framed within its (post)-colonial context, and alternative histories and voices should be privileged to address the imbalance" (P37, a White faculty member from the UK). This is a theme to which we return in Chap. 7.

Theme 6.4: Decoloniality as Counter-erasure
Decoloniality can also be a radical move that involves a counter-erasure: "Decoloniality, to me, means unwhite-washing everything. It means to repaint everything on the canvas that's white with a broad multi-hued brown brush. The annihilation of white institutions, white systems, white ways of saying and doing everything" (P90, a Black PhD candidate from North America). Here it is evident that the dehumanising effects that resulted from colonialism, creating a wretched of the earth (Fanon 1963) can be overturned as the former colonial subjects take up their agency to erase, delink and heal from the colonial wound (Mignolo 2011). There

seems to be no place for inclusion of White knowledge in this response. This theme was not prevalent in the responses of other participants but it is important to note that not every participant is thinking along the lines of inclusion of all types of knowledge.

Theme 6.5: Decoloniality as an Invisible Notion
A few participants, both lecturers and students, indicated that they had not heard of the notions of transformation and decoloniality nor of any potential links between the two: "Never heard transformation linked to decolonisation" (P198, an Asian student from Japan) and "Don't know, not sure" (P8, a White academic in the Netherlands), "these notions are too new and vague" (P264, a White student in Germany) and "I'm not familiar with these ... terms" (P105, a White academic in Germany). The concepts may be unknown because decoloniality is a more common term in some contexts, and because transformation is not widely used with reference to decoloniality beyond South Africa. However, unfamiliarity with neither concept is somewhat troubling as the discourses of decolonisation and decoloniality are circulating in large parts of academia in many parts of the world, but clearly not everywhere equally. One participant felt that something needed to be done about the lack of knowledge: "Honestly, I don't know. But I feel like I have a sort of civil responsibility to know" (P222, a White postgraduate student in South Africa). A core issue for South African students during the student movements was decolonisation of the curriculum yet this student of linguistics remains unaware of these issues while expressing that they feel obliged to know.

Theme 6.6: A New Metalanguage for the Study of African Linguistics
Linked to processes of undoing and (re)doing is finding a new metalanguage for the study of African linguistics. This would involve putting "African languages in an equal stance with other languages" (P2, an Asian faculty member in Japan) and "Moving beyond teaching grammatical functions to discourse functions in African languages. Study African languages on [… their] own terms" (P11, a Black faculty member in Malawi). This would excavate deeper knowledges in African languages beyond a reductionist approach and constitute a reading of the African world and word (Freire 1985).

The benefits of this new metalanguage would be multiple with students being able to "Study in (their) mother tongue" (P14, a White faculty member in South Africa) and "if our African languages could be used we would understand better in lectures ... we cannot even use our languages to ask questions or answer ..." (P21, a Black academic in South Africa). Languages also have agency: "African languages to decolonise our institutions in Africa" (P21, a Black student in South Africa). This may gel with Ruiz's (1984) language-as-resource orientation. However, these responses take it beyond language-as-resource, and object only, to show how bodies experience language and intersections within domains in the academy (van der Merwe 2022). Languages would become more visible and students may experience access and success "if some of the courses or programmes were taught in an African language, some of the African students would benefit and perform well" (P211, a mixed race faculty member in South Africa). Significantly the curriculum would "become more inclusive and representative of the people (and their experiences) of the republic (not just in terms of race but also of gender, class etc.)" (P215, a Black faculty member in South Africa). This references the pluriverse discussed in Theme 6.3 above.

There is caution about a decolonial project that "aims to eliminate Afrikaans as far as possible, ultimately to the detriment of African languages in general" (P217, a White postgraduate student in South Africa). In terms of this response, a metalanguage should include Afrikaans. Afrikaans is a South African language which is associated with colonialism and apartheid but which to some is also a language that has been undone and redone by Black and Brown South Africans and therefore part of decolonisation. This participant clearly considers Afrikaans an African language which may be uncontroversial among linguists but somewhat contested in South Africa society more generally. It is a language with varieties that have been both resisted, especially during the Black student uprising in 1976 in South Africa, but also in the recent student movements. These movements resulted in Afrikaans being removed as language of teaching and learning at several South African universities. There is a wariness and ambivalence about the role of Afrikaans in a decolonised canon.

Theme 6.7: Decoloniality and Positionality
Two White participants referenced their own positionality and alluded to the intersectionality of marginalised female academics when engaging with the concept of coloniality. They sought to veer away from defining

decoloniality as P81, a White faculty member in Germany, states that "Being White myself, I cannot even imagine what it means to be a woman of colour in this system". A further response is about a "Need to be more humble considering our privileges as White researchers" (P224, a White postgraduate student in Germany). An intersectional lens needs to be used to discuss experiences of Black women in the academy, whose experiences are ignored and marginalised (Gabriel and Tate 2017), in a reconsideration of transformation and decoloniality. Self-reflexivity was seen as needed in the decolonial project with the "adoption of serious, meaningful reflexivity in everyone's daily practice – especially in terms of examining positionality, thinking about wider and long-term impacts of actions" (P84, a White academic in the Netherlands).

Theme 6.8: Decoloniality as Self-serving
Some of our participants noted that discussions around decoloniality and transformation may not result in real or sustained change. The idea of decoloniality as self-serving with a focus on theory not praxis came up a number of times, ranging from the conceptual underpinnings, to performative 'fake' actions.

Decoloniality as praxis is not being realised according to some participants and "decoloniality exists in theory and not practically" (P94, a Black student in South Africa). One reason put forward by P113 (an Asian academic in Japan) for this is that:

> Transformation is a useful concept involving changing societal structures (education included) to become more inclusive and representative ... Decolonization is less useful, I find, because it is so heavily contested and because its more public proponents have done such a good job of making it seem idiotic and trivial ... and – in the worst cases – self-serving "(e.g. linguists who use it as a tool to discredit the linguistic disciplines of others while arguing that (coincidentally) their discipline is the only one true way)."

These contestations have often revolved around what decoloniality is and is not, for example whether it constitutes soft reform, radical reform or beyond-reform (Zembylas 2018) or if it is a passing trend (Jansen 2019). There could also be a pushback against decoloniality to hold onto canons that have long been sacrosanct. This leads to a superficial and hollow words approach where much is said but little done to change the status quo: "an amazing unwillingness within institutions for change and all calls for 'diversity, inclusion, equity' are mostly lip service" (P81, a White faculty member in Germany). The structures that were established to drive Global South studies come under examination with some doing better than others: "[a research focused institution in Europe] seems to, at least superficially, do a better job of discourse on decolonisation, but it could be better incorporated into the actual business process of the university" and "Understanding the history of [the institution] and why it was established" (P200, a White student in Germany).

Theme 6.9: Decoloniality and Entrenched Global North Power
In the participants' responses, several actions were proposed to dislodge entrenched Global North powers. These include "supporting African academics in my subfield and empowering them to carry out research in the face of their own limited institutional support' (P116, a White academic in the United States). A troubling subtheme that arises here though is the African academic as an object of empowerment. Another concern raised is that "The field is still dominated by White researchers and that there is a need for more diversity. We need to listen more and give space to researchers from African countries. And not only space for doctoral positions. Also the professorships" and "the field is still dominated by White researchers. There is a need for more diversity" (P224, a White postgraduate student in Germany). Though the appointment of researchers needs to go hand in hand with decolonial ontological and epistemological stances of appointees. One intriguing response related to the digital was that "Technology invisibilises African languages even more" (P189, a Black academic in Nigeria). This could be in reference to digital divides and inequalities on the continent and the limited space occupied digitally by African knowledges.

The resistance to inclusion of Global South knowledge because of an apparent lack of expertise can be seen in P200's responses: "As students in [an institution in Europe] we fought for more representation of African languages beyond the linguistic context, but the professors were not really on board … they said they weren't qualified to teach such classes" and that, therefore, "The Africa department in [European city] is definitely in need of decolonising, they seemed to hide behind the 'objectivity' of linguistics and we never had a proper discourse on the problematic history of our institute (former colonial institute)." The decolonial project is seen as extending beyond epistemology to the historical structures of institutions. Mbembe (2015) speaks of pedagogies of presence and how Black academics need to engage in creative acts that make it impossible to be ignored. It also is inclusive of methodologies used in the Global South "I heard of research that is conducted in African countries without the researchers ever learning to speak the language" (P200).

Theme 6.10: Resistance to Decoloniality
A discourse that is also prevalent is that of decoloniality, resistance, opportunism, and pushback against the very core of its ideals because "There is a feeling that if you engage with ideas of decolonisation then you are painting a target on your back because whatever you do will never be good enough and you will always be criticised by the very same people who promote decolonisation – the revolution eats its children" (P215, a Black faculty member in South Africa). The implication being that decolonisation equates to substandard academic ways of being. There is also a perception of duplicity where some may talk of decoloniality but in their actions support the status quo. To some respondents there is opportunism with it being seen as a "problem (and) used by people with very different agendas and often those agendas are hateful" (P215). The impact of this is on epistemology and it has become "tainted in this way (and therefore) very difficult to engage seriously with" (P215).

Furthermore, decoloniality has become elitist with "an elite that takes it onto itself to tell everybody else what decolonization must mean and to also define the telos – the end – to which it aspires" (P215). For this participant decoloniality may be unattainable, especially with "the chaos and misunderstanding of what it is" (P215). The pushback can come from White students in Linguistics classes as "African languages in class (is) offensive to White students. The use of African languages in class creates divisions" (P139, a White academic in North America) while (P225, a White student in Germany) sees decolonisation as "only relevant for institutions in Africa". Resistance to decolonising is thus seen in different spaces by the participants, also due to contestations about meanings.

6.3 Summary and Reflections

This chapter examined discourses on decoloniality and transformation. Transformation was viewed as a process with decoloniality as an outcome. However, several respondents also saw transformation as a process in its own right. The two concepts were also conflated and used synonymously in participant responses. Many participants were more familiar with the concept of decoloniality than transformation. As discussed in Chap. 1 transformation is a discourse prevalent in South Africa, more so than in other countries, and this came through in engagement with the term. Despite this, even though transformation is more used in South Africa, many participants from other parts of the globe were also familiar with the term and saw its connections to decoloniality.

The survey responses were all embedded in perceptions of what counts as decoloniality and transformation and where African linguistics finds itself. The complexity of narrowing down definitions of decoloniality, how to best situate decoloniality and (un)doing and (re)doing decolonial work in colonial structures, what Mbembe (2015) calls anachronistic structures and the enduring hegemony of Eurocentric canons, all emerged from the responses. Contestations around who does decolonial work and why with resultant pseudo-decolonial practices, also emerged.

The positionality of Whiteness in a decolonial project was briefly alluded to in a number of responses but not unpacked. Besides the knowledge project, there were strong feelings about the need for a dismantling of colonial structures in the Global North. How African languages are presented is seen as needing to move away from a Western gaze of validation. The under-representation of the Global South in the research methodologies also came under the spotlight. There were calls for theorising to stop and for doing to take centre stage. In a climate of Global Otherness and after a long period of theorising, a decolonial 'doing moment' is emerging, and is indeed needed, as is reflected in participant responses.

References

Dilraj, Isha. 2021. Race, transformation and education as contradictions in a neoliberal South Africa. *The Thinker* 86: 1–11. https://doi.org/10.36615/thethinker.v86i1.448.

Fanon, Frantz. 1963. *The wretched of the earth.* Trans. Richard Philcox. New York: Grove Press.

Freire, Paulo. 1985. Reading the world and reading the word: An interview with Paulo Freire. *Language Arts* 62: 15–21. National Council of Teachers of English.

Gabriel, Deborah, and Shirley Anne Tate, eds. 2017. *Inside the ivory tower: Narratives of women of colour surviving and thriving in British academia.* London: Trentham Books.

Habib, Adam. 2013. *Reflections of a university bureaucrat interested in advancing a progressive social agenda.* Kagisano. Number 9. The Aims of Higher Education. CHE.

Jansen, Jonathan D., ed. 2019. *Decolonisation in universities: The politics of knowledge.* Wits University Press. https://doi.org/10.18772/22019083351.

Makalela, Leketi. 2016. Ubuntu translanguaging: An alternative framework for complex multilingual encounters. *Southern African Linguistics and Applied Language Studies* 34: 187–196.

Mamdani, Mahmood. 2019. Decolonising universities. In *Decolonization in universities: The politics of knowledge*, 15–28. Johannesburg: Wits University Press.

Mbembe, Achille. 2015. Decolonizing knowledge and the question of the archive. Wits Institute for Social and Economic Research.

———. 2019. Future knowledges and their implications for the decolonisation project. In *Decolonization in universities: The politics of knowledge*, 239–254. Johannesburg: Wits University Press.

van der Merwe, Chanel. 2022. Re-considering orientations in south African language policies. *Bandung* 9: 279–299. https://doi.org/10.1163/21983534-09010011.

Metz, Thaddeus. 2011. Ubuntu as a moral theory and human rights in South Africa. *African Human Rights Law Journal* II(2): 532–559.

Mignolo, Walter D. 2011. Epistemic disobedience and the Decolonial option: A manifesto. *TRANSMODERNITY: Journal of Peripheral Cultural Production of the Luso-Hispanic World* 1. https://doi.org/10.5070/T412011807.

Mignolo, Walter D., and Catherine E. Walsh. 2018. *On Decoloniality: Concepts, analytics, praxis.* On Decoloniality. Durham, NC: Duke University Press.

Muthien, Bernedette, and June Bam. 2021. *Rethinking Africa: Indigenous women re-interpret southern Africa's pasts.* Johannesburg: Jacana Media.

Ndlovu-Gatsheni, Sabelo. 2013. Why decoloniality in the 21st century? University of Johannesburg. *The thinker* 48. 10–5. https://hdl.handle.net/10210/470999.

Ngũgĩ wa Thiong'o. 1986. *Decolonising the mind: The politics of language in African literature*. London: James Currey.

Ruiz, Richard. 1984. Orientations in Language Planning. *NABE Journal*, 8(2): 15–34. https://doi.org/10.1080/08855072.1984.10668464.

Zembylas, Michalinos. 2018. Decolonial possibilities in south African higher education: Reconfiguring humanising pedagogies as/with decolonising pedagogies. *South African Journal of Education* 38: 1–11. https://doi.org/10.15700/saje.v38n4a1699.

Open Access This chapter is licensed under the terms of the Creative Commons Attribution 4.0 International License (http://creativecommons.org/licenses/by/4.0/), which permits use, sharing, adaptation, distribution and reproduction in any medium or format, as long as you give appropriate credit to the original author(s) and the source, provide a link to the Creative Commons license and indicate if changes were made.

The images or other third party material in this chapter are included in the chapter's Creative Commons license, unless indicated otherwise in a credit line to the material. If material is not included in the chapter's Creative Commons license and your intended use is not permitted by statutory regulation or exceeds the permitted use, you will need to obtain permission directly from the copyright holder.

CHAPTER 7

Conclusions, Next Steps and a Call to Action

Abstract This chapter constitutes a conclusion to the book as a whole. It highlights patterns and insights that emerge from the data on which our study is based, as well as the broader context in which the work is situated. This chapter considers ongoing issues related to African languages in higher education, including the erasure of African languages, as well as the power of African languages and their role in movements for change. The chapter reminds us that racist assumptions which still underlie the study of African languages need to be rooted out and addressed in instructional contexts. This includes the erasure and/or absence of African languages from university spaces, including classrooms and curricula. However, the necessity and impact of such actions in the classroom will also necessarily vary according to context. It concludes with a call for continued action and a warning that true decolonisation must go beyond theory, and must instead be enacted and practised in order to ensure meaningful and lasting change.

Keywords African Languages • Educational spaces • Positionality • Erasure • Empowerment • Prominence

7.1 Overview

In this short book we have explored issues related to African languages and linguistics, and transformation and decolonisation. We have used the findings of an online survey carried out in 2021 as the basis of the exploration of these issues. The original survey aimed to examine the views of students and instructors on these issues, both within and outside Africa. The study, in part, arose from some of our observations and experiences as educators and researchers, based in Africa, working on African languages, or thinking about the link between linguistics and social justice and change.

The survey was also inspired by the work of de Vos and Riedel (2023) who surveyed South African linguistics and language instructors and departments. Their survey found that while instructors reported being involved in curriculum transformation, many of these efforts remained partial and/or of varied success and depth. Their study also highlighted that some of the efforts may have been viewed as tokenistic—a theme that emerged in the present study as well. Similarly, their observations gave rise to further questions related to how best to support instructors to make meaningful changes to their curricula and teaching practice where individual instructors determine their own curriculum decisions, as well as how best to ensure truly decolonised curricula and teaching contexts. These are also themes which we identified and explored in the current study.

7.2 Key Findings and Observations

7.2.1 African Languages in Higher Educational Spaces

Our findings in Chap. 3 suggest that a large proportion of our respondents were at institutions where African languages are taught. However, we are aware that this probably does not reflect the broader picture across institutions and countries, since it is likely that a higher proportion of our respondents were based at these types of institutions given that they chose to engage with and complete the survey.

A proportion of both students and instructors did not respond to the question about whether African languages were taught at their institutions or said that they did not know. It is difficult to develop a more fine-grained interpretation of this since we do not have comparative data on other languages or language groups and this was not the focus of our study.

However, we also wonder whether the relative erasure and marginalisation of African languages plays into the number here. To put it differently, if we had asked respondents whether European languages were taught at their institutions, would we have had a different response? Either in terms of greater prominence, a clearer idea of what might constitute European languages and/or would it have been the same as this is based on respondents' understanding of the teaching and learning options at their institutions?

One of the areas that was most informative here related to the open-ended responses we received about people's experiences of African languages in higher education. Here some noted that studying an African language had fundamentally changed their worldviews as well as career trajectory. Others commented that the teaching of African languages had—or could—improve cultural understanding and facilitate exchange between groups and individuals. The more negative responses primarily related to the teaching of African languages, broader support and the way in which the teaching of these languages is under-developed in some respondent's views. It is therefore not that African languages are taught that is criticised here, but more the broader context and perhaps style/quality of the way in which some of the languages are taught.

Respondents also commented on the respective positionality of African languages compared to other languages—European/Western languages in particular—in both higher education and more broadly. Others also highlighted the need for there to be a diversity of opportunities to encounter, learn and be exposed to African languages. Those based in Africa commented that people should be exposed to African languages from an early age, while noting the importance of African languages in higher education, including in carrying out research for example. Finally, some respondents did comment that any experiences they had had with African languages were entirely distinct and distant from their academic study, highlighting perhaps the importance of the wider contexts but also that higher education was not an environment in which African languages were centred.

7.2.2 *The Erasure of African Languages from Higher Educational Spaces*

Our findings highlight a greater degree of prominence than showing erasure as such, in part no doubt due to how the questions were framed. While some respondents noted that only a few classes featured African language examples, most of our respondents focused on what was visible, noteworthy and/or memorable. This was the case for both students and instructors, although the perspectives and observations were naturally somewhat different between the groups.

We think the picture overall is somewhat skewed towards greater prominence, seeing as a large number of types of linguistics classes were mentioned and a relatively high diversity of African languages were named explicitly. But we do not know if they were only mentioned once or twice in a semester, only in passing or exoticised or otherwise marginalised. What does come out quite strongly is the intention or self-reported action by faculty members to include African languages in their teaching. This theme in particular calls for further examination in a detailed follow-up study, employing semi-structured interviews. It was exactly these types of insights we were interested in better understanding when we developed the survey and started exploring these issues.

7.2.3 The Link Between African Languages and Decolonisation/Transformation

In terms of the role of African languages in the higher education classroom, in Chap. 5 we explored how various positionalities, institutional, linguistic, and geographic, might shape respondents' perspectives on the role of teaching African languages and decolonisation/transformation efforts. The findings suggest that we cannot make sweeping claims about the role of African languages as part of decolonisation efforts without taking into account the context of students, instructors and institutions. However, as we describe in further detail below, these responses and actions must take place in their appropriate local context. Those instructors who are more personally removed from the experience of being colonised overall had different perspectives on the role of teaching/learning African languages in decolonisation efforts from those instructors whose classrooms are located in a context where students grew up using African languages. Students themselves had a more positive view, and connected increased attention to African languages in the classroom to material benefits for African language users outside of the classroom.

The survey was in part motivated by the student- and early career scholar-led social movements that have taken place across contexts and institutions. Our team was initially interested in differences between students and faculty in terms of their perceptions about the role of African languages in decolonisation and transformation processes. In addition, we also carried out this research with our own experiences in mind as to how an instructor's intent is not always clear in practice, along with some degree of scepticism of how much simple inclusion can lead to transformative changes. However, it became clear that the positionality of the respondent with respect to African languages, whether these languages are ones that they grew up with or languages which they study as outsiders to the community, can and should influence our interpretation of these responses. As such, we also asked how use of African languages and location might predict the valence of responses to the question of what role there might be for African languages in decolonisation and transformation efforts.

From a pedagogical perspective, instructors should keep in mind that the potential value of contextualised inclusion of African languages in linguistic curricula for undergraduate students, particularly in Africa, may be significant for undergraduates who grew up using these languages and seeing them devalued. Outside of Africa, the potential material benefits to language users seem to be understated as compared to the benefits for linguists or linguistics. Overall, making transparent the potential connections between including African languages in linguistic curricula and decolonisation/transformation could go a long way to understanding points of (dis)connection between students and instructors.

Racist assumptions which continue to underlie the study of African languages need to be rooted out and addressed in instructional contexts, and the necessity and impact of such actions in the classroom will vary according to context. Tokenistic inclusion is harmful, but instructors need not let their critical impulses obscure the potential and perceived value for students. Further, as seen in Chap. 6, negative valence or resistance to African languages as a part of transformation/decolonisation practices cannot be interpreted simplistically. In our survey, resistance comes both from those who would like to see more concrete, widespread, lasting changes, as well as those who are resistant to the idea of decolonisation/transformation as a concept. Critique and rejection, in other words, must be addressed and interpreted differently.

7.2.4 *Understandings of Decolonisation and Transformation*

We also explored respondents' understandings of transformation and decolonisation. Findings show that the two concepts are not names for the same thing and that transformation is often seen as a broad change that in some instances encompasses decolonisation. The concept of transformation is more prevalent in South African national higher education policy documents post-democracy where it has adopted a role as a specific type of broad ranging change.

Decoloniality as a term and concept is familiar to most of our participants although two participants did indicate that they had never heard of decoloniality. Understandings of decoloniality involved it as subject with agency to dislodge Eurocentrism and make visible erased knowledge. It was viewed as something that can ameliorate a canon that wounds. However, many respondents felt that decoloniality was stuck in a morass of theory, as some noted the difference between "talking decoloniality and walking decoloniality". Others also noted that it had remained largely a theoretical notion and the wide-ranging reforms and whole-scale systematic change that many expected has not taken place.

Positive comments alluded to the humanity that decoloniality can foster between people and between groups. There were also extensive responses about processes which seek to undo and redo knowledge. It was suggested that this would lead to the development of a new language of description. There was however, resistance and pushback. Respondents warned of the need to guard against opportunism, tokenism, and surface-level change.

7.3 Directions for Future Research

The use of an online survey to carry out the original survey naturally brings with it a number of limitations. We were not able to follow up with respondents to better understand their responses, the people who completed the survey were naturally only those who we had been able to access via our personal and professional networks, and the survey design meant that some parts were more "fully" completed than others. However, we designed and circulated the survey during the height of the Covid-19 pandemic and as such, being able to carry on with this at a time when there were limits of travel and conducting face-to-face research does mean that we were able to carry on with survey which we might have had to pause or abandon completely if we had opted for a different methodology. The use of an online survey also meant that we were able to get responses from people based in different countries and across a relatively broad geographic area.

In terms of possible directions for future research, exploring some of the responses and emerging patterns through the use of different methodologies would be a natural next step. It would be great to be able to conduct short semi-structured interviews with people to gain deeper insights into views on the role and place of African languages and linguistics, as well as the link between these and decolonisation and transformation. All of the key questions that motivated the original survey and that we explored in the present volume, would benefit from conversations and interviews with respondents.

Similarly, the distribution of respondents in terms of geographic location, career stage/role, and other demographic categories is random, given the way in which we distributed the survey. A systematic approach would be needed if we wanted to address imbalances in our respondents' profile, as well as if we wanted to attempt any form of representativeness in the responses and the respondents. Another potential avenue for future research would be to target specific disciplines and courses to better understand the use and representation of African languages in these areas, both within linguistics and in non-language related courses.

Finally, one of the key goals of publishing the works and sharing our findings is to survey as a prompt—and hopefully inspiration—for others to also explore similar and related issues, in teaching and in research, as well as the broader physical spaces that higher education institutions offer and constitute.

7.4   Where to from Here?

This monograph is not meant as a guidebook or a 'How to' manual. However, in presenting the findings, and highlighting perceptions about the links between African languages and decolonisation/transformation, we have sought to interrogate some of the invisible and visible legacies which continue to shape our disciplines and discourses on African languages and African linguistics as a field.

Recent years have seen the growth of movements calling on educational and research institutions around the world to acknowledge their role in shaping assumptions about racial and global hierarchies. As individuals based in higher education institutions in the United States, UK and South Africa, we have been involved in these discussions and the work that is necessary for this to take place. In this short book, we have taken the 2015 #RhodesMustFall movement as a lens through which to explore these issues, as well as a critical touchpoint for social justice movements, linked to and housed in universities and colleges the world over. The movements are distinct but, in many cases, linked by common concerns and issues. A central and uniting feature shared by many of the movements is to call into question the ways in which academic disciplines have shaped our thinking about the world, what constitutes legitimate topics of study and appropriate methodological approaches, and how to appropriately produce and share knowledge.

As academics working in the fields of linguistics and language, as well as educators, we are committed to the reforms that we believe need to take place in our disciplines, our institutions and academia more widely. We are committed to continuing to be involved in the campaigns, discussions and discourses that are needed for the change to take place. We continue to educate ourselves, work with colleagues and students, and to question our roles, positionalities and responsibilities in regard to the ongoing work of shaping our institutions and higher education more broadly.

This survey started from a particular historical moment in which we found ourselves interested about the movements that were taking place, but also committed to contributing to the change and carrying it forward. We took #RhodesMustFall as a crucial moment in this period of time. We wanted to highlight the marginalisation of African languages that we had encountered in our own learning, teaching and research contexts. We wanted to better understand the experiences of others in this regard, as well as to see whether we would be able to identify examples of good practice and suggestions that could be shared more widely. Ultimately, the way we conducted the research and the responses that we received were much more about experiences, views and opinions than about sharing of best practice. But we consider this to be an important insight and finding. We believe that the patterns that emerged from the current study show that there is perhaps much more background and preparatory work to be done. Changes that we might consider to be essential to the better embedding of African languages within the broader decolonial turn and decolonising work still needs to happen. But there is no singular way in which this can be carried out, either between or within individual contexts.

Finally, we cannot make generalised claims such as "learning about African languages is a central part of colonisation efforts". However, it does seem that our starting point that African languages operate from a position of historical and continued marginalisation means that the potential for the teaching of African languages and linguistics to be involved in overturning and addressing the colonial legacies in linguistics and higher education more broadly remains under explored. In some ways, we found less 'erasure' of African languages than we expected. But we also found ourselves asking whether this was because people were so used to this, because people did not expect to find African languages in these spaces that they did not notice that they were missing. Any change that takes place needs to be meaningful and embedded within both the broader and more localised context. We remain conscious of tick-box or surface-level attempts at reform, which, as noted by some of our respondents, might be tokenistic or do more harm than good.

It is our aim to continue to explore—and be involved in the shaping of—our disciplines with a view to addressing the racist and imperialised historical legacies that are found in our institutions, our disciplines, our teaching and our research. We believe that African languages have a central role to play in this. We believe that social justice movements have a central role to play in this. If decoloniality represents an 'undoing' of the erasure, and the epistemic violence that has been done, then the role of language in this can not be underestimated. Because indeed it is the very thing that shapes our ideas, the ways we communicate about our pasts and our presents, the way we communicate about our realities, and the way that we implement change in places that need to change.

We continue to follow the evolution of African linguistics after #RhodesMustFall, in South Africa, in our respective contexts and globally. We continue to give and attend talks, we continue to review our curricula and to encourage our colleagues to do the same. We continue to interrogate our teaching practices, and our research and research methodologies. It is not enough to talk about decoloniality, we must also "walk decoloniality".

In this way, we must ourselves also ensure that we do not fall into the trap of talking about these issues, sharing views on these issues but not doing the underlying work that is needed to bring African languages and African languages to the front and centre of a decolonised and transformed curricula. In this work and in our day-to-day lives, we draw on our experiences of doing research and teaching languages spoken in colonised and colonising contexts. We draw on our experiences as individuals and as a collective to contribute to shaping a decolonised and transformed educational experience for our students, as well as building decolonised and transformed institutions. Working together, we reflect on the importance of solidarity in work of this nature. We believe that there is great power in working together, both in the ways in which we can support each other and share experiences and resources, and in the ways that we can continue to push each other and find energy to interrogate the issues that continue to lie at the heart of our work. We continue to call on our educational and research institutions, as well as our disciplines and sub-disciplines to acknowledge their role in shaping assumptions about racial and global hierarchies. As we were so crucially reminded by one of the respondents to our survey "Decolonisation is doing. It has been theorised to death." We must continue to act, and continue to do.

Reference

De Vos, Mark, and Kristina Riedel. 2023. Decolonising and transforming curricula for teaching linguistics and language in South Africa: Taking stock and charting the way forward. *Transformation in Higher Education* 8. https://doi.org/10.4102/the.v8i0.200.

Open Access This chapter is licensed under the terms of the Creative Commons Attribution 4.0 International License (http://creativecommons.org/licenses/by/4.0/), which permits use, sharing, adaptation, distribution and reproduction in any medium or format, as long as you give appropriate credit to the original author(s) and the source, provide a link to the Creative Commons license and indicate if changes were made.

The images or other third party material in this chapter are included in the chapter's Creative Commons license, unless indicated otherwise in a credit line to the material. If material is not included in the chapter's Creative Commons license and your intended use is not permitted by statutory regulation or exceeds the permitted use, you will need to obtain permission directly from the copyright holder.

Appendix

The survey comprised the following 26 questions, in addition to asking participants for their consent to be part of the study and for their data to be used.

Demographic/Biographical Details

Q1: Which country are you based in? (if you regularly move between countries, please provide brief details).

Q2: Which countries have you spent a significant amount of time in (more than 6 months)?

Q3: What is your current academic role?

Q4: What is your highest educational qualification/degree?

Q5: How would you describe yourself in terms of race/ethnicity?

Q6: I identify my gender as...

Q7: Did you grow up using an African language or languages? Which one(s)?

Q8: Were African languages used in your home or in surrounding areas where you grew up? If so, which one(s)?

ACADEMIC DETAILS

Q9: What kind of department(s) are you studying or teaching in (e.g. general linguistics, applied linguistics, history, African languages, politics/ political science, African studies, language department)?

Q10: Answer one or both of the following questions as relevant: If you are currently studying for a degree: What is your degree title or major and level/year (BA, BA Honours, MA, MPhil, PhD, EdD, etc.)?

Q11: If you are an instructor: What degree programme(s) are you teaching in (if you are teaching on a non-degree programme, please also indicate here)?

How are African languages and ways of thought incorporated into your teaching and learning

Q12: Are African languages taught at your university/institute? If yes, which language or languages?

Q13: Are you studying or have you studied an African language? If yes, which ones? What motivated your decision to study this language/these languages?

Q14: What courses are offered at your institution that relate specifically to African languages?

Q15: Are there examples from African languages in the class/es you teach?

Q16: If there are examples from African languages in the class/es you teach or study, which classes do they appear in? And what languages are the examples from (mention as many as seem relevant).

Q17: If so, in what context or how is this used?

Q18: Where else in your education (for example in other classes, research group meetings, talks on campus etc.) have you learned about or been exposed to African languages?

Q19: What do the notions of transformation or decoloniality mean to you?

Different academic contexts and countries use different terms for this. However, the visibility and place of African languages and linguistics is often seen as part of a broader need to decolonise or in some countries the need to transform higher education or more generally achieve a greater level of equity and inclusivity. We're curious what these terms mean to you, either in abstract, in practice, or both.

Q20: What do you consider to be the link between the presence of African languages/linguistics at universities and processes of decolonisation/transformation?

Q21: Can you give examples of decolonisation, teaching for social justice or transformation that you have participated in in linguistics or language learning contexts?

Q22: What might decolonisation, teaching for social justice or transformation look to you in practice in language and/or linguistics classes?

Q23: What role do you think studying and learning about African languages plays in processes of decolonisation, teaching for social justice or transformation of higher education?

Q24: In your own local context, are African philosophies, ways of thinking or theories (particularly those on linguistics) and examples included in what is presented as the linguistics 'canon' (i.e. what is presented as the "core" of linguistics)?

Q25: Is there anything else about your experience with African languages that you would like to share?

Q26: Do you have any questions or comments for the survey team?

References

Adli, Aria, and Gregory R. Guy. 2022. Globalising the study of language variation and change: A manifesto on cross-cultural sociolinguistics. *Language and Linguistics Compass*. 16: 5–6. https://doi.org/10.1111/lnc3.12452.

Ahmed, Sara. 2007. 'You end up doing the document rather than doing the doing': Diversity, race equality and the politics of documentation. *Ethnic and Racial Studies* 30: 590–609. https://doi.org/10.1080/01419870701356015.

———. 2012. *On being included: Racism and diversity in institutional life*. Durham: Duke University Press.

Alexander, Neville. 1989. *Language policy and National Unity in South Africa/Azania*. Cape Town: Buchu Books.

Andrews, Kehinde. 2020. The challenge for black studies in the neoliberal university. In *Decolonising the university*, ed. Gurminder K. Bhambra, Kerem Nişancıoğlu, and Dalia Gebrial, 129–144. London: Pluto Press.

Anthym, Myntha, and Franklin Tuitt. 2019. When the levees break: The cost of vicarious trauma, microaggressions and emotional labor for black administrators and faculty engaging in race work at traditionally white institutions. *International Journal of Qualitative Studies in Education* 32: 1072–1093. https://doi.org/10.1080/09518398.2019.1645907.

Arndt, Jochen S. 2023. Zulu vs Xhosa: How colonialism used language to divide South Africa's two biggest ethnic groups. *The Conversation*. May 11. https://theconversation.com/zulu-vs-xhosa-how-colonialism-used-language-to-divide-south-africas-two-biggest-ethnic-groups-204969.

Badat, Saleem. 2016a. *Black student politics: Higher education and apartheid from SASO to SANSCO, 1968–1990.* New York: Routledge. https://doi.org/10.4324/9781315829357.

———. 2016b. Deciphering the meanings, and explaining the south African higher education student protests of 2015–16. *Pax Academica* 1 (1): 71–106.

Bhambra, Gurminder K., Kerem Nişancıoğlu, and Dalia Gebrial. 2018. *Decolonising the university.* London: Pluto Press.

Borja, Melissa, Russel Jeung, Aggie Yellow Horse, Jacob Gibson, Sarah Gowing, Nelson Lin, Amelia Navins, and Emahlia Power. 2020. *Anti-Chinese rhetoric tied to racism against Asian Americans stop AAPI hate report.* Asian Pacific Policy & Planning Council.

Boveda, Mildred, and Subini Ancy Annamma. 2023. Beyond making a statement: An intersectional framing of the power and possibilities of positioning. *Educational Researcher.* https://doi.org/10.3102/0013189X231167149.

Breetzke, Gregory D., and David W. Hedding. 2018. The changing demography of academic staff at higher education institutions (HEIs) in South Africa. *Higher Education* 76: 145–161.

Brown, David, and Teri Del Rosso. 2022. Called, committed and inspiring activism: How black PR guest speakers experienced the PR classroom during the COVID-19 and racial reckoning academic year of 2020/2021. *Journal of Public Relations Education* 8 (2): 42–77.

Bucholtz, Mary, and Abdesalam Soudi. 2020. Creating more just and inclusive learning experiences linguistic society of America webinar series: Racial justice, equity, diversity, and inclusion in the linguistics curriculum.

Burkhard, Tanja. 2022. Facing post-truth conspiracies in the classroom. A black feminist autoethnography of teaching for liberation after the summer of racial reckoning. In *Departures in critical qualitative research*, vol. 11, 24–39. University of California Press. https://doi.org/10.1525/dcqr.2022.11.3.24.

Calhoun, Kendra. 2021. *Competing discourses of diversity and inclusion: Institutional rhetoric and graduate student narratives at two minority serving institutions.* UC Santa Barbara, PhD dissertation.

Calhoun, Kendra, Jamaal Muwwakkil, Rachel E. Weissler, Joyhanna Yoo Garza, and Savithry Namboodiripad. 2023. *Linguists' reflections on responses to the 'racial reckoning' of 2020 in U.S. higher education: A collective conversation on lessons learned and next steps presented at the 2023 Linguistic Society of America Annual Meeting.* Boulder, CO.

Cele, G., and C. Koen. 2003. Student politics in South Africa: A study of key developments. *Cahiers de la recherche sur l'éducation et les savoirs* 2: 201–223.

Charity-Huddley, Anne H., Christine Mallinson, and Mary Bucholtz, eds. 2024. *Decolonising Linguistics.* Oxford: Oxford University Press.

Chetty, Rajendra, Hannah Gibson, and Colin Reilly. 2024. Decolonising methodologies through collaboration: Reflections on partnerships and funding flows from working between the 'south' and the 'north'. In *Decolonizing linguistics*, ed. Anne H. Charity Huddley, Christine Mallinson, and Mary Bucholtz. Oxford: Oxford University Press.

Clark, Brad. 2022. *Journalism's racial reckoning: The news media's pivot to diversity and inclusion*.

Collart, Aymeric. 2024. A decade of language processing research: Which place for linguistic diversity? *Glossa Psycholinguistics* 3 (1). https://doi.org/10.5070/G60111432.

Colombetti, Giovanna. 2005. Appraising valence. *Journal of Consciousness Studies* 12: 103–126.

Council on Higher Education. 2021. *Vital stats: Public higher education 2019*. Pretoria: Council on Higher Education.

Davids, Nuraan, and Yusef Waghid. 2016. History of South African student protests reflects inequality's grip. *The Conversation*. October 9. https://theconversation.com/history-of-south-african-student-protests-reflects-inequalitys-grip-66279.

De Vos, Mark, and Kristina Riedel. 2023. Decolonising and transforming curricula for teaching linguistics and language in South Africa: Taking stock and charting the way forward. *Transformation in Higher Education* 8. https://doi.org/10.4102/the.v8i0.200.

De Vos, Mark, Kristina van der Merwe, and Caroline van der Mescht. 2014. A research Programme for Reading in African languages to underpin CAPS. *Journal for Language Teaching*. 48 (2): 143–171.

Department of Education. 2001. *National plan for higher education*. Pretoria: Department of Education.

Department of Higher Education and Training. 2013. *White paper for post-school education and training: Building an expanded, effective and integrated post-school system*. Pretoria: Department of Higher Education and Training.

Deumert, Ana, and Nkululeko Mabandla. 2017. Beyond colonial linguistics: The dialectic of control and resistance in the standardization of isiXhosa. In *Standardizing minority languages*, ed. Pia Lane, James Costa, and Haley de Korne, 200–221. New York: Routledge.

Diemer, Maxine, Kristin van der Merwe, and Mark de Vos. 2015. The development of phonological awareness literacy measures for isiXhosa. *Southern African Linguistics and Applied Language Studies* 33 (3): 325–341.

Dilraj, Isha. 2021. Race, transformation and education as contradictions in a neo-liberal South Africa. *The Thinker* 86: 1–11. https://doi.org/10.36615/thethinker.v86i1.448.

Eberhard, David M., Gary F. Simons, and Charles D. Fennig, eds. 2023. *Ethnologue: Languages of the world*. 26th ed. Dallas, TX: SIL International.

Evans-Winters, Venus E., and Pamela Twyman Hoff. 2011. The aesthetics of white racism in pre-service teacher education: A critical race theory perspective.

Race, Ethnicity and Education 14: 461–479. Routledge. https://doi.org/10.1080/13613324.2010.548376.

Exeter, CIGH. 2016. Leopold must fall. *Imperial & Global Forum*. https://imperialglobalexeter.com/2016/06/28/leopold-must-fall/. Accessed 30 July 2024.

Falola, Toyin. 2020. The Ibadan School of History. In *From ivory towers to ebony towers transforming humanities curricula in South Africa, Africa and African-American studies*, ed. Oluwaseun Tella and Shireen Motala, 211–227. Johannesburg: Jacana Media.

Fanon, Frantz. 1963. *The wretched of the earth*. Trans. Richard Philcox. New York: Grove Press.

Freire, Paulo. 1985. Reading the world and reading the word: An interview with Paulo Freire. *Language Arts* 62: 15–21. National Council of Teachers of English.

Gabriel, Deborah, and Shirley Anne Tate, eds. 2017. *Inside the ivory tower: Narratives of women of colour surviving and thriving in British academia*. London: Trentham Books.

Garton, Paul. 2021. Types of anchor institution initiatives: An overview of university urban development literature. *Metropolitan Universities* 33: 85–105. https://doi.org/10.18060/25242.

Garza, Alicia. 2014. A herstory of the #BlackLivesMatter movement. *The Feminist Wire*. October 7.

Gebrial, Dalia. 2020. Rhodes must fall: Oxford and movements for change. In *Decolonising the university*, ed. Gurminder K. Bhambra, Kerem Nişancıoğlu, and Dalia Gebrial. London: Pluto Press.

Gibson, Hannah, Kyle Jerro, Savithry Namboodiripad, and Kristina Riedel. 2024. Towards a decolonial syntax: Research, teaching, publishing. In *Decolonizing linguistics*, ed. Anne H. Charity Huddley, Christine Mallinson, and Mary Bucholtz. Oxford: Oxford University Press.

Govender, Prega. 2016. #FeesMustFall cost 18 varsities more than R460m in damage to property alone. *Mail and Guardian*. October 10. https://mg.co.za/article/2016-09-29-00-feesmustfall-cost-18-varsities-more-than-r460m-in-damage-to-property-alone/.

Güldemann, Tom. 2014. 'Khoisan' linguistic classification today. In *Current issues in linguistic theory*, ed. Tom Güldemann and Anne-Maria Fehn, vol. 330, 1–40. Amsterdam: John Benjamins Publishing Company. https://doi.org/10.1075/cilt.330.01gul.

Habib, Adam. 2013. *Reflections of a university bureaucrat interested in advancing a progressive social agenda*. Kagisano. Number 9. The Aims of Higher Education. CHE.

Hammonds, Evelyn M. 2021. A moment or a movement? The pandemic, political upheaval, and racial reckoning. *Signs: Journal of Women in Culture and*

Society 47: 11–14. The University of Chicago Press. https://doi.org/10.1086/715650.

Heath, Helen, and Sarah Cowley. 2004. Developing a grounded theory approach: A comparison of Glaser and Strauss. *International Journal of Nursing Studies* 41: 141–150. https://doi.org/10.1016/S0020-7489(03)00113-5.

Ho, Jennifer. 2021. Anti-Asian racism, black lives matter, and COVID-19. *Japan Forum* 33: 148–159. https://doi.org/10.1080/09555803.2020.1821749.

Hou, Lynn, and Kristian Ali. Critically examining inclusion and parity for deaf global south researchers of colour in the field of sign language linguistics. In *Inclusion in linguistics*, ed. Anne H. Charity Hudley, Christine Mallinson, and Mary Bucholtz. Oxford University Press. https://doi.org/10.1093/oso/9780197755303.003.0003.

Jansen, Jonathan D., ed. 2019. *Decolonisation in universities: The politics of knowledge*. Wits University Press. https://doi.org/10.18772/22019083351.

Jansen, Jonathan D., and Cyrill A. Walters. 2022. *The decolonization of knowledge: Radical ideas and the shaping of institutions in South Africa and beyond*. Cambridge: Cambridge University Press. https://doi.org/10.1017/9781009082723.

Kanigel, Rachele. 2016. White, white. *Diversity Style Guide*. April 12.

Kidd, Evan, and Rowena Garcia. 2022. How diverse is child language acquisition research? *First Language* 42 (6): 703–735. https://doi.org/10.1177/01427237211066405.

Li, Yao, and Harvey L. Nicholson. 2021. When "model minorities" become "yellow peril"—Othering and the racialization of Asian Americans in the COVID-19 pandemic. *Sociology Compass* 15: e12849. https://doi.org/10.1111/soc4.12849.

Makalela, Leketi. 2016. Ubuntu translanguaging: An alternative framework for complex multilingual encounters. *Southern African Linguistics and Applied Language Studies* 34: 187–196.

Mamdani, Mahmood. 2019. Decolonising universities. In *Decolonization in universities: The politics of knowledge*, 15–28. Johannesburg: Wits University Press.

Maseko, Pamela. 2018. Rethinking Africa series: Whose history counts: Decolonising African pre-colonial historiography. In *Language as source of revitalisation and reclamation of indigenous epistemologies*. Cape Town: Sun Media.

Mbembe, Achille. 2015. Decolonizing knowledge and the question of the archive Wits Institute for Social and Economic Research.

———. 2019. Future knowledges and their implications for the decolonisation project. In *Decolonization in universities: The politics of knowledge*, 239–254. Johannesburg: Wits University Press.

Mbembe, Achille, Olivier Mongin, Nathalie Lempereur, Jean-Louis Schlegel, and John Fletcher. 2006. What is postcolonial thinking? *Esprit*: 117–133.

van der Merwe, Chanel. 2022. Re-considering orientations in south African language policies. *Bandung* 9: 279–299. https://doi.org/10.1163/21983534-09010011.

Mignolo, Walter D. 2011. Epistemic disobedience and the Decolonial option: A manifesto. *TRANSMODERNITY: Journal of Peripheral Cultural Production of the Luso-Hispanic World* 1. https://doi.org/10.5070/T412011807.

Mignolo, Walter D., and Catherine E. Walsh. 2018. *On Decoloniality: Concepts, analytics, praxis. On Decoloniality*. Durham, NC: Duke University Press.

miles-hercules, deandre, Jamaal Muwwakkil, and Kendra Calhoun. 2020. *Racial justice, equity, diversity, and inclusion in the linguistics curriculum: This IS linguistics: Scope, positionality, and graduate apprenticeship when diversifying linguistics curriculum*. Invited talk for a pedagogy webinar put on by the Linguistic Society of America.

Moore, Julia E., Brian K. Bumbarger, and Brittany Rhoades Cooper. 2013. Examining adaptations of evidence-based programs in natural contexts. *The Journal of Primary Prevention* 34: 147–161. https://doi.org/10.1007/s10935-013-0303-6.

Morris, Aldon. 2020. The Atlanta School of Sociology. In *From ivory towers to ebony towers transforming humanities curricula in South Africa, Africa and African-American studies*, ed. Oluwaseun Tella and Shireen Motala, 342–356. Auckland Park: Jacana Media.

Muehlhausen, Beth L., Cate Michelle Desjardins, Beba Shensi Tata-Mbeng, Christa Chappelle, Allison DeLaney, Antonina Olszewski, Csaba Szilagyi, and George Fitchett. 2023. Spiritual care department leaders' response to racial reckoning in 2020 and 2021. *Journal of Health Care Chaplaincy*: 1–15. https://doi.org/10.1080/08854726.2023.2167416.

Muthien, Bernedette, and June Bam. 2021. *Rethinking Africa: Indigenous women re-interpret southern Africa's pasts*. Johannesburg: Jacana Media.

Muwwakkil, Jamaal, Kendra Calhoun, J. Garza, Savithry Namboodiripad, and R. Weissler. 2023. *Reflections on responses to the 'racial reckoning' of 2020 in U.S. higher education: A collective conversation on lessons learned and next steps*. Webinar sponsored by the American Education Research Association Language and Social Processes Special Interest Group. Online.

Namboodiripad, Savithry, and Nathan Sanders. 2020. *Centering linguistic diversity and justice in course design*. Presented at the Linguistic Society of America webinar series: Racial Justice, Equity, Diversity, and Inclusion in the Linguistics Curriculum. August 14.

Namboodiripad, Savithry, Corrine Occhino, and Lynn Hou. 2019. *A survey of linguists and language researchers: Harassment, bias, and what we can do about it*. Plenary panel presented at the 93rd Annual Meeting of the Linguistic Society of America, New York City.

Nash, Margaret A. 2019. Entangled pasts: Land-Grant colleges and American Indian dispossession. *History of Education Quarterly* 59: 437–467. Cambridge University Press. https://doi.org/10.1017/heq.2019.31.

Ndlovu-Gatsheni, Sabelo. 2013. Why decoloniality in the 21st century? University of Johannesburg. *The thinker* 48.

Ngũgĩ wa Thiong'o. 1986. *Decolonising the mind: The politics of language in African literature*. London: James Currey.

Pennycook, Alastair, and Sinfre Makoni. 2020. *Innovations and challenges in applied linguistics from the global south*. Routledge.

Pillow, Wanda. 2003. Confession, catharsis, or cure? Rethinking the uses of reflexivity as methodological power in qualitative research. *International Journal of Qualitative Studies in Education* 16: 175–196. https://doi.org/10.1080/0951839032000060635.

Probert, Tracy, and Mark de Vos. 2016. Word recognition strategies amongst isiXhosa/English bilingual learners: The interaction of orthography and language of learning and teaching. *Reading & Writing* 7 (1). https://doi.org/10.4102/rw.v7i1.84.

Ray, Victor E., David Luke, Antonia Randolph, and Megan Underhill. 2017. Critical race theory, afro-pessimism, and racial Progress narratives. *Sociology of Race and Ethnicity* 3 (2): 147–158. https://doi.org/10.1177/2332649217692557.

Reddy, Thiven. 2004. *Higher education and social transformation: South Africa case study*. Johannesburg: Council for Higher Education.

Robertson, Rebecca. 2023. A critical race theory analysis of transnational student activism, social media counter-stories, and the hegemonic logics of diversity work in higher education. *International Journal of Qualitative Studies in Education* 36: 900–917. https://doi.org/10.1080/09518398.2021.1885073.

Satyo, Sizwe. 1992. A response to Neville Alexander's essay: 'Language policy and National Unity in South Africa/Azania'. *Southern African Journal of Applied Language Studies* 1 (1): 41–50. https://doi.org/10.1080/10189203.1992.9724591.

Secules, Stephen, Cassandra McCall, Joel Alejandro Mejia, Chanel Beebe, Adam S. Masters, Matilde L. Sánchez-Peña, and Martina Svyantek. 2021. Positionality practices and dimensions of impact on equity research: A collaborative inquiry and call to the community. *Journal of Engineering Education* 110: 19–43. https://doi.org/10.1002/jee.20377.

Smith, Patriann. 2022. Black immigrants in the United States: Transraciolinguistic justice for imagined futures in a global metaverse. *Annual Review of Applied Linguistics* 42: 109–118. https://doi.org/10.1017/S0267190522000046.

Stein, Sharon. 2020. A colonial history of the higher education present: Rethinking land-grant institutions through processes of accumulation and relations of conquest. *Critical Studies in Education* 61: 212–228.

Thomas, Kevin D., Judy Foster Davis, Jonathan A.J. Wilson, and Francesca Sobande. 2020. Repetition or reckoning: Confronting racism and racial dynamics in 2020. *Journal of Marketing Management* 36: 1153–1168. Routledge. https://doi.org/10.1080/0267257X.2020.1850077.

Tuck, Eve, and K. Wayne Yang. 2012. Decolonization is not a metaphor. *Decolonization: Indigeneity, Education & Society* 1: 1–40.

Universities South Africa. 2015. *Reflections on higher education transformation discussion paper*. Prepared for the second national Higher Education Transformation Summit.

Witzlack-Makarevich, Alena, and Hirosi Nakagawa. 2019. Linguistic features and typologies in languages commonly referred to as 'Khoisan'. In *The Cambridge handbook of African linguistics*, ed. H. Ekkehard Wolff, 382–416. Cambridge University Press. https://doi.org/10.1017/9781108283991.012.

Wright-Mair, Raquel, and Kara Ieva. 2022. Are we in this alone? Examining the cost of Health & Wellness by surviving the neoliberal academy for multiple Minoritized faculty. *Journal of Trauma Studies in Education* 1: 1–29. https://doi.org/10.32674/jtse.v1i1.3648.

Zembylas, Michalinos. 2018. Decolonial possibilities in south African higher education: Reconfiguring humanising pedagogies as/with decolonising pedagogies. *South African Journal of Education* 38: 1–11. https://doi.org/10.15700/saje.v38n4a1699.

Index[1]

NUMBERS AND SYMBOLS
#RhodesMustFall, 1–17, 37, 39, 97, 115–117

A
Academia, 12, 16, 24, 25, 27–30, 32, 35, 77, 83–84, 88, 100, 116
African linguistics, 1–17, 32, 51, 62, 66, 92–105, 110, 115, 117
Afrikaans, 8, 33, 39, 40, 53, 57, 66, 68, 69, 77, 101
Afrolatinx, 94
Apartheid, 4, 6, 7, 35, 39, 40, 52, 78, 97, 101
Arabic, 32, 66
Awarding gap, 11

B
Bantu languages, 3, 3n1, 34, 36, 39, 64, 65, 67–69
Black Lives Matter, 11, 12
Black students, 6, 7, 9, 56, 96, 97, 101, 102

C
Cameroon, 26, 65
Canada, 94
Canon, 39, 92–94, 98, 99, 101, 102, 105, 114
Caribbean, 26
Colonial academy, 92
Coloniality/colonisation, 3n1, 5, 10, 37, 82, 88, 96, 98, 101, 116
Colonial languages, 33, 65
Covid-19, 2, 9, 12, 114

---

[1] Note: Page numbers followed by 'n' refer to notes.

© The Author(s) 2025
H. Gibson et al., *African Linguistics after #RhodesMustFall*,
https://doi.org/10.1007/978-3-031-74817-2

Curriculum, 2–4, 4n1, 6–12, 34, 35, 39, 63, 64, 70, 78, 88, 93–95, 100, 101, 110

D

Decoloniality/decolonisation, 1–6, 6n2, 8–10, 13, 14, 16, 24, 25, 27, 30, 31, 34, 35, 37–41, 44, 49, 55, 63, 64, 72, 76–89, 92–105, 110, 112–115, 117, 118
Discourse, 3, 5, 6, 6n2, 10, 12, 16, 17, 24, 35, 38, 39, 52, 57, 83, 91–105, 115, 116

E

East Africa, 37, 79
Empire, 3, 97
Equity, 4, 6, 35, 36, 64, 92, 95, 103
Equity and Diversity Committee, 12–13
Erasure, 2, 41, 46, 57–59, 61–72, 94, 111–112, 117
Eurocentric, 6, 10, 98, 105
Europe, 2, 10, 15, 26, 49, 51, 57, 67, 78, 81–83, 86, 87, 103

F

Faculty, 7, 12, 27, 28, 30, 32, 37, 38, 45–48, 50, 57, 58, 62, 65–70, 76–84, 87–89, 94–104, 112
French, 15, 32, 56, 65

G

Gender, 25, 30–32, 95, 101
Germany, 37, 55, 70, 95, 100, 102–104
Ghana, 98

Global North, 10, 93, 94, 96, 97, 99, 103, 105
Global South, 10, 38, 98, 99, 103–105

H

Hegemony, 36, 56, 77, 96, 105
Higher education, 2, 4–11, 15, 16, 24, 25, 30, 33–35, 37–39, 41, 43–59, 61–72, 76, 77, 80, 92, 96–98, 111, 112, 114–117

I

Inclusive pedagogy, 13
Inequality, 2, 5, 9–11, 34, 57, 96, 103
Instructor, 3, 4, 9, 13, 27, 28, 47, 61, 62, 66–71, 78, 83, 88, 89, 110, 112, 113
Ireland, 97

K

Kenya, 26
'Khoisan,' 3, 3–4n1, 14, 62, 65–67
Knowledge, 5, 10, 35, 39, 41, 46, 47, 49–51, 54, 80, 83, 92–100, 103, 105, 114, 116

L

Linguistics, 1–17, 24, 25, 32, 34–37, 39, 40, 44, 45, 49, 51–54, 62–72, 63n1, 78, 80, 81, 83, 85, 89, 92–105, 110, 112, 113, 115–117
Linguistic Society of America, 12, 36

M

Morphology, 62, 66, 67, 70, 71

INDEX

N
Neocolonialism, 38
Netherlands, 71, 97, 100, 102
Nigeria, 26, 65, 103
North America, 2, 10, 13, 15, 26, 27, 36, 48–49, 55, 66, 69, 76, 78, 79, 81, 87, 89, 96, 98, 99, 104

P
Participants, 4, 6n2, 8, 13–15, 24–33, 36, 38, 45, 61–64, 66, 67, 70–72, 76, 77, 82, 84–88, 92–96, 100–105, 114
Phonetics, 62, 63, 70, 71
Phonology, 63, 66, 69–71
Positionality, 15, 16, 33–41, 49, 59, 81, 85, 88, 94, 101, 102, 105, 111–113, 116
Post-colonialism, 80, 93
Postgraduate students, 27, 49, 54, 55, 62, 94, 96, 100–103
Professional organisations, 12

R
Race, 5, 25, 30–32, 34, 40, 54, 55, 69, 77, 95, 101
Racialised disadvantage, 10, 11, 34, 37
Racial reckoning, 2, 10–14
Racism, 2, 3, 5–7, 80
Rhodes, Cecil, 5, 11–12

S
Scotland, 10, 94
Social change, 2, 4, 46, 77
Solidarity, 77, 79, 95, 117
South Africa, 3–15, 26, 31, 33–40, 48, 50, 52–57, 63, 66–70, 72, 77, 78, 80, 81, 95–97, 99–102, 104, 105, 115
South African English, 33
South America, 26
Staff, 5–8, 11, 16, 30, 37–41, 43–59, 62, 69
Student protests, 6–9
Survey, 1–4, 4n1, 6n2, 10, 11, 13–16, 23–41, 43–45, 47, 48, 58, 62–72, 76, 84, 88, 92, 93, 96, 98, 105, 110, 112–116, 118
Swahili, 15, 37, 40, 62, 64–67, 70, 71
Syntax, 4, 5, 63, 63n1, 66, 67, 70, 71

T
Tanzania, 26, 37
Teaching materials, 3, 63
Tokenised, 88
Transformation, 1–9, 6n2, 13, 14, 16, 24, 25, 27, 30, 31, 34, 37, 39–41, 44, 49, 55, 63, 64, 72, 76–89, 92–105, 110, 112–115

U
Ubuntu, 93, 95
Ubuntu translanguaging, 93
Undergraduate students, 27, 28, 50, 56, 62, 69, 77, 80, 82, 86, 88, 89, 113
Under-representation, 2, 11, 105
Undoing and (re)doing, 94, 96–100, 105, 117

W
West Africa, 53, 79
Whiteness, 32, 105
White students, 7, 11, 57, 78, 95, 97, 98, 100, 103, 104

The manufacturer's authorised representative in the EU is Springer Nature Customer Service Centre GmbH, Europaplatz 3, 69115 Heidelberg, Germany. If you have any concerns regarding our products, please contact ProductSafety@springernature.com

Printed and bound by CPI Group (UK) Ltd, Croydon, CR0 4YY
23/03/2026
02076355-0005